P9-DEG-515

Antwerp & Ghent

Footprint

Clare Thomson

Contents

Listings

About the author

After several hectic months criss-crossing Estonia, Latvia and Lithuania as communism collapsed around her – an experience that formed the basis of her first book, *The Singing Revolution: A Political Journey through the Baltic States* – Clare Thomson moved to the relative calm of Brussels, where she worked as a journalist throughout the 1990s. Since returning to London, she has worked on several guides to Belgium, as well as Footprint's *Tallinn* pocket guide, and written about Flanders and further afield for, among others, the *Independent* and the *Sunday Times*. She can name any number of famous Belgians but, after fighting with the endless Flemish variants of Dutch, she has had to concede that being able to order *grijzenoordzeegarnalen* is as good as it's ever going to get.

Acknowledgements

Huge thanks to Matthew for childcare, bar-crawl companionship and expertise in the field of Belgian stoner rock, to Rosa and Ella for sightseeing with (some) enthusiasm, to my Mum, Ingrid Thomson, and to Nana Trish and Grandpa Mike. Heartfelt thanks also to Raymond Bogaert, Kathleen Cagney, Jeff Davidse, Frank Deijnckens and the Antwerp Tourist Office, Pit de Jonge, Ronnie Dusoir, the Flanders Tourist Office in London, the Ghent Tourist Office, Peter Haex, Stefan Hertmans, Ellen Hubert, Tom Lanoye, Guido Latre, Vik Leyten, Dirk Luyten, Tom Nagels, Dominique Piedfort, Anne Provoost, Martin Raud, Het Roze Huis, the Vanden Broecke family, Herman van Dromme and Carine Wijffels, Leen van Dyck and the Letterenhuis, and Ann Willems.

Introducing Antwerp and Ghent

Antwerp may be Belgium's second city, but for the locals, it is the centre of the universe. Antwerpenaars are almost rabidly proud of their multifaceted city and are swift to remind you that this is the home of Rubens, the diamond capital of the world and a fashion centre to rival Paris and Milan; that its sprawling port is Europe's second largest, and that it has more bars per head than any other city in the world. The good news is, their pride is not misplaced: the city on the Scheldt marks the point where Latin and Germanic cultures connect, and offers a beguiling and sometimes bizarre blend of both worlds. It's a hard city to pin down, not least because so many areas vie for your attention: beyond the historic centre, with its gabled guild houses and baroque beauties, there's the fashion district, the museums of the ultra-trendy Zuid, the atmospheric old marinas in 't Eilandje and the pick-and-mix architectural insanity of the Zurenborg. Wherever you wind up, you'll be assured of a mind-blowing meal and endless opportunities to acquaint yourself with Trappist ales.

On the waterfront

As the local saying has it, "Antwerp has God to thank for the Scheldt, and the Scheldt to thank for everything else". For 1000 years or more, the river has been the key to the city's prosperity. Even the name is thought by some to derive from '*aan de werpen*', or 'on the wharf'. Although Antwerp isn't on the sea, the Scheldt estuary is wide enough to take even the largest vessel, and has been ever since the 16th century, when Antwerp was Europe's most prosperous and dynamic city. All that was to change in 1648, when the Treaty of Münster resulted in the closure of the river, plunging Antwerp into a depression that lasted 200 years. When the city regained full control of the Scheldt in 1863, Antwerp bounced back with a vengeance, expanding the docks north of the city centre, then, as the size of ships increased, moving further down the river. Today, the port and its warehouses and processing plants cover 140 sq km.

Grand designs

It cannot be a coincidence that the Dutch word '*ontwerp*' means 'project', as Antwerpenaars have long had a fondness for ambitious architectural plans. The cathedral spire was for centuries the tallest in the Lowlands; the Boerentoren was Europe's first serious skyscraper; and the city now has a new eco-friendly law court designed by Richard Rogers. Antwerp sees itself as the most dynamic and prestigious city in Belgium, but its planners often bite off more than they can chew, for example at the vast building site that is the Koningin Astridplein.

The 'vision thing' is not limited to the city planners, either. Restaurant design has become an art in itself, especially in 't Eilandje, where there are some staggering warehouse and factory conversions. The same goes for the city's shops: Walter Van Beirendonck's flagship, a former garage, has an astounding interior by the uber-designer Marc Newson. And in the grungier bars across town, you'll find a host of would-be poets and authors, ready to start on their magnum opus as soon as they've had that next drink…

Antwerp at a glance

Although the second-largest city in Belgium, with a population of 450,000, Antwerp is reasonably compact and easy to explore on foot. The river forms a natural boundary on one side of the city centre; on the other, there's the inner ring, a series of boulevards known as the Leien. The names (Britselei, Amerikalei et al) recall the allied powers who fought for Belgium's freedom in the First World War.

Historic centre

Defined by the first, long-destroyed city walls and, on its western edge, by the river, Antwerp's historic core fans out around the Gothic cathedral, the Renaissance town hall and the brooding Steen castle. Though both world wars have left their mark, the area is dotted with baroque churches and Gothic guild houses, eloquent reminders of the days when this was one of Europe's most influential cities. The medieval street pattern is pleasantly perplexing, especially for visitors absent-mindedly gazing at gables, or lost in admiration of a secret alley or courtyard.

St Andries and the Latin Quarter

This atmospheric neighbourhood, south of the historic centre, is named after pretty St Andrew's Church. Traditionally the home of the poor – it was once known as the 'parish of misery' – it has come up rapidly in the world in recent years, and is now the hub of Antwerp's white-hot fashion scene. There are scores of designer boutiques on Lombardenvest, Kammenstraat and Nationalestraat (where you'll also find MoMu, an excellent fashion museum). The main attraction in the once-dubious Latin Quarter is the Rubenshuis, where the city's greatest son lived and worked for almost three decades; Sunday brunch beneath the elegant rotunda of the Bourla theatre's café runs it a close second.

Diamond and Jewish districts

Antwerp may be the diamond capital of the world, but the security-heavy streets on which the big deals are brokered are anything but glamorous. You can learn at least some of the secrets of the world's most precious stone at the Diamond Museum, but if it's glitz you're after, you'll find it in the astoundingly opulent Centraal station and the architectural follies in the city's zoo, one of the world's oldest. Southeast of the station, you enter the Jewish area, home of the black-clad, homburg-sporting Chassidic community – and of Hoffy's, one of Europe's finest kosher kitchens.

Het Zuid

Almost too glamorous for its own good, 'the South' feels like a gigantic backdrop for a glossy magazine shoot, with swish restaurants, chi-chi design stores and achingly trendy bars and cafés lining the filled-in quays at the district's heart. Thankfully, there's substance as well as style, with Van Eyck, Rubens and Ensor canvases on show at the Fine Arts Museum, and cutting-edge contemporary art at the Muhka. It's a fine spot for a summer stroll, too, with handsome town houses assembled around an elegant star-shaped street pattern.

't Eilandje

North of the centre, the 'Little Island' takes its name from the bridges, docks and marina that seem to cut it off from the rest of the city. This was once the heart of the harbour, but the need for deeper docks saw it fall into disrepair. After decades of neglect, it's being recast as the destination of choice for lovers of the loft-living lifestyle, with spectacular warehouse conversions housing apartments and some of the city's most ambitious restaurants. It still has plenty of true grit, though, especially in the southern Schipperskwartier, once a rough seamen's haunt and now home to the legalized red-light district.

Zurenborg

The star turn in this southeastern neighbourhood is the
remarkable array of almost neurotically overwrought belle
époque villas that line Cogels-Osylei and the surrounding streets.
Tudor beams, Venetian loggias, Greek statuary, art nouveau:
you name it, the architects have copied it, and sometimes all
in the same building. The district's name, 'Acid Town', refers not
to the bitchy bourgeoisie who commissioned these colossal
confections, but to the quality of the local soil. On the other
side of the railway tracks is Dageraadplaats, a laid-back,
ethnically diverse – and yes, café-lined – square.

Borgerhout

This once-thriving industrial district east of Centraal station
hit hard times in the 1970s, but is slowly regaining its pride.
Dismissively dubbed 'Borgerocco' by right-wingers, a reference
to the large Moroccan population, it has its grim stretches, but
cheap rents are drawing artists and bohos in ever greater
numbers, and there are some keynote attractions: the EcoHuis,
a showcase for sustainable living; Panamarenko's purpose-built
gallery; and De Roma, an art deco cinema revived as one of the
city's best concert venues.

Antwerp trip planner

24 hours in Antwerp

There's only enough time to scratch the surface, so stick between
the Scheldt and the inner ring. Start with a visit to the **Cathedral**,
then cut east to the plush **Rockoxhuis**. Return to the **Grote
Markt** via serene **Hendrik Conscienceplein** and the creeper-
strewn houses of **Wijngaardstraat**, then have a coffee (or beer)
as you admire the statue of Silvius Brabo and the fine Renaissance
guild houses. From here, you have a choice of routes to the chi-chi
and culture-rich **Zuid**: via the easy-going antiques shops and

★ Antwerp: 10 of the best

Best

1   Cathedral of Our Lady You'll see the spire from all corners, but the close-up view is breathtaking – as are the Rubens paintings inside, p34.

2   Hendrik Conscienceplein The city's stateliest square, with its proud patrician mansions and a beautiful baroque church, p46.

3   Rockoxhuis Relive the glory days of Antwerp in the luxuriously appointed home of its early-17th-century mayor, a friend and patron of Rubens, p48.

4   St Anna Tunnel What lies beneath: an art deco foot tunnel leads under the Scheldt, with sweeping views from the other side, p53.

5   Plantin-Moretus Museum This atmospheric mansion retains the presses and proofing desks from its 16th-century heyday as Europe's publishing powerhouse, p54.

6   MoMu An absolutely fabulous fashion museum, just a few steps from the shops, p56.

7   Mayer van den Bergh Museum From Bruegels to breviaries, this turn-of-the-century private collection is small but perfectly formed, p66.

8   Royal Museum of Fine Arts Big building, big names: Van Eyck and Rubens are the stars, Ensor and Wouters are the revelations, p78.

9   Cogels-Osylei Two millennia worth of architectural styles, one sublimely ridiculous street, p91.

10 Middelheim Sculpture Park Sunday in the park with Henry, Barbara and Auguste at this superlative sculpture garden, p95.

The ★ symbol is used throughout the guide to indicate these recommended sights.

bohemian brasseries of **Kloosterstraat**; or via **Nationalestraat**, with detours into **Sint-Andries** for a spot of designer shopping. Once in the Zuid, check out Rubens and his compatriots at the **Fine Arts Museum** on Leopold de Waelplaats, or head to the Vlaamse Kaai for the **FotoMuseum** and contemporary art at **Muhka**. A short tram ride takes you back to the centre for drinks and dinner; or stay in the Zuid and carouse until dawn.

A long weekend in Antwerp (2-4 days)

Simply by stopping at every bar that takes your fancy, you could stretch the above itinerary to two days. Or three. But there is plenty more to see if you have time, starting with the atmospheric, UNESCO-listed **Plantin-Moretus Museum**, on the fringes of the fashion district. Hang out on the waterfront and visit the **Vleeshuis** and the medieval **Steen**, and take the pedestrian tunnel beneath the Scheldt for the panoramic view from the other side of the river. Head out towards Centraal station for the **diamond district**; don't forget **Rubenshuis**; and go south for the treasures of the **Mayer van der Bergh Museum**. A late-afternoon stroll along the old harbours of **'t Eilandje** will leave you well placed for dinner; or take a tram to the wedding-cake mansions of **Cogels-Osylei** or gritty but intriguing **Borgerhout**. If the weather's decent, a visit to the **Middelheim Sculpture Park** is a must.

Introducing Ghent

Ghent tends to be overlooked by tourists as they rush to play sardines on the cobbled streets of Bruges: but more fool them, as this former medieval powerhouse is far more than a museum town. It shares with Bruges a dreamy combination of gabled houses, willow-lined waterways and slender spires – in fact, as the locals delight in pointing out, there are more listed monuments in the city centre than in any other Belgian town – but has a grittier, more urban feel, and the presence of about 50,000 students brings with it nightlife to rival Antwerp's. There's a local obsession with heaven and hell – you'll spy impish devils or ecstatic angels atop the gables, while allusions to paradise lost, forsaken or regained appear in the names of eateries and B&Bs – and a canal walk on a misty autumn morning comes with a delicious frisson of spookiness.

Rebel rebel

The citizens of Ghent have long been renowned for their stubborn, anti-authoritarian streak, and it's caused them no end of trouble. They backed the English in the Hundred Years' War, only to be crushed by the French; in 1453, after a failed tax rebellion against Philip the Good, Duke of Burgundy, the city's dignitaries were forced to parade with nooses around their necks; then, in the 1530s, they repeated the tax trick, this time cocking a snook at Charles V. Though Charles was born in Ghent, he showed little mercy, knocking down an ancient abbey and replacing it with a citadel. Still, the locals refused to submit, siding with the Calvinists during the wars of religion – only to fall to the Spanish in 1584.

Jenny genie

Fast-forward two centuries, and Ghent's indomitable spirit resurfaces – but this time in a less belligerent manner. In 1800, Lieven Bauwens spirited a spinning jenny out of Britain and established the city's first mill. The trend caught on, and Ghent became one of Europe's leading textiles centres. In the face of low pay and dreadful conditions, the workers soon united, sowing the seeds of a socialist tradition that remains strong today: in 2003, the city witnessed Belgium's first same-sex marriage; condom-sellers are allowed into its car parks at night; it was the first place in the country to introduce rickshaw taxis; and it has a long-standing progressive pedestrianization policy (with only the occasional rumble of a tram to obscure the sound of bicycle bells and rippling carillons).

24 hours in Ghent

Start at **St Bavo's Cathedral**, aiming to get to the *Lamb of God* before everyone else does. If you're feeling fit, clamber up the 300-odd steps of the **Belfry**, for clanging carillons and views over Flanders fields, then head to **Sint-Michielsbrug** for a sight of the city's dreamy spires. Linger over a coffee on the **Graslei**, then visit the imposing **Gravensteen** for a rampart ramble. Interiors addicts should make for the **Museum voor Sierkunst**, then lunch at **Jan Breydelstraat**; homespun types might prefer the **Kinderen Alynsgodshuis**, then a potter through the restaurant-laden **Patershol**. In the afternoon, head south for the consummate art collections of **Smak** and (from 2007) the **Fine Arts Museum**, or for a stroll in the serene **Citadelpark**, returning to the centre for dinner and a moonlit waterside wander.

A long weekend in Ghent (2-4 days)

Ghent's cobbled streets and canals are made for leisurely strolling, with plenty of pit stops at the city's bars and cafés. That said, there's plenty more to see: down south, **Sint-Pietersabdij** offers evocative insights into the Benedictine abbey's often turbulent history, the **Vooruit** is an elegant example of fin-de-siècle eclecticism and, on Sundays, the **Kouter** hosts a flamboyant flower market; up north, **MIAT** is a shrine to industrial architecture, the **Bijloke Museum** potters amiably through Ghent's past and the **Dr Jozef Guislain Museum** puts mental illness under the microscope. If the weather's good, take a boat tour or hire a bike and trek out along the leisurely curves of the Leie to leafy **Sint-Martens-Latem**, inspiration for two generations of Flemish artists and a perfect picnic spot.

Alternatively, go back to your student rhythm, sleep through the daytime and spend all your nights drinking, dancing or both: rockers, ravers and ruminators will all find their niche.

★ **Ghent: 10 of the best**

Best

1 Adoration of the Mystic Lamb The undisputed highlight of St Bavo's Cathedral – indeed, one of the greatest medieval artworks – Jan Van Eyck's exquisite 1432 altarpiece has a history as colourful as its oil-painted panels, pp100-102.

2 Sint-Michielsbrug The view of Ghent's three towers – stout St Bavo's, the soaring Belfort and stern, sober St Nicholas – is so good, they built a bridge to observe it from, p104.

3 Graslei/Korenlei The heart of the medieval port, with the river running through an assemblage of Romanesque, Gothic, Renaissance and baroque buildings. Graslei has the finer architecture, Korenlei the better view, p105.

4 Gravensteen There's been a castle here since the ninth century: its current incarnation may not be authentically medieval, but it certainly looks that way, p107.

5 Museum voor Sierkunst If recreated Regency rooms, exquisite art nouveau and quirky contemporary creations aren't enough, how about the world's most eye-catching public convenience? p108.

6 Kouter Join the locals for oysters, champagne and brass-band standards at the fragrant Sunday flower market, p110.

7 Sint-Pietersabdij Meet a monk who's taken a shine to single malts on an innovative interactive tour of this handsome baroque abbey, p111.

8 SMAK Bend your brain over Beuys and Bruce Nauman at one of Europe's finest contemporary art museums, p112.

9 Kinderen Alynsgodshuis A charming old almshouse with a bloody past, now home to a genuinely fascinating folklore museum, p117.

10 Dr Jozef Guislain Museum Named after a pioneering psychiatrist, a showcase for 'outsider' art and a frank exploration of attitudes to mental illness down the ages, p118.

Contemporary Antwerp

A Belgian city that's cool? Journalists on both sides of the Atlantic have been frantically trying to square that particular circle in recent months, singing the praises of Antwerp as the ultimate 'lifestyle destination' while trying to relocate it in '21st-century Europe' or the Free Republic of *Wallpaper**.

Most of it's nonsense, of course – but they have stumbled on an interesting paradox in this most paradoxical of cities. Though Antwerp is quintessentially Belgian in myriad ways – from its grimy streets to the shrimp croquettes and beery stews on so many of the menus – a good proportion of its citizens regard the motherland with distaste and outright suspicion. They see Antwerp as the flagship city of an independently-minded Flanders (although, in a typical instance of Belgian political sleight of hand, francophone Brussels is the official capital of Flanders) and many would like to sever all ties with the French-speaking regions.

More complex still, the nature of that state is the hottest issue in town right now. On the surface, Antwerp is avant-garde, progressive and endlessly creative, ready to embrace and set new trends in culture, food or fashion. (Where else would a Catholic priest commission designer clothes for a statue of the Virgin Mary?) But it has a darker side: the strong level of support for the extreme-right Vlaams Belang, whose separatist, racist policies have struck a chord with as many as one in three Antwerpenaars, could see the VB seize control of the city council in the October 2006 elections.

To understand how this came to be, we have to delve through the history of this proud but strangely insecure port city. It's been a cosmopolitan melting pot for more than five centuries, yet has long had a reputation for not welcoming outsiders, or only putting up with them because, sometimes, it makes commercial sense to do so. It was among the world's most powerful cities in the 16th century, but has endured long periods of stagnation and misery, breeding a sense of introspection and insecurity. Where Holland is uncomplicatedly Protestant, patriotic and ever so slightly predictable, Catholic Flanders, and Antwerp in particular, is more Latin, more mysterious, restless and constantly surprising.

Antwerpenaars have never been afraid to talk up their city's potential but, until the mid-1980s, most outsiders would have seen it as a backwater. Then the 'Antwerp Six' took the international fashion scene by storm, and people began to look anew at the city. At the same time, developers began to snap up the disused quays and warehouses that lined the river, a much-needed shot in the arm for the local economy. As Glasgow did in 1990, Antwerp enjoyed a triumphant reign as Europe's Cultural Capital in 1993, and it has been on a roll ever since. A leading Flemish writer, Tom Lanoye, encapsulates the sudden change in Antwerp's fortunes. In his 1988 novel *Everything Must Go*, the narrator fulminates about this "city of past jazz triumphs, of bygone hippiedom and days of yore. Fat city, flabby city, heart attack and liver disease... The Bruges of the 20th century." Today, Lanoye, who served as the first city poet, admits that he is constantly amazed by how vibrant and 'cool' Antwerp has become.

There is a downside to this rush of prosperity and civic pride, however: the idea that bullish, buoyant Flanders is being held back by the rest of Belgium, in particular the French-speaking region, Wallonia, where heavy industry has taken a nosedive in recent decades. Many Flemings resent the fact that part of their income goes on propping up the Walloon economy – and the Vlaams Belang party is happy to play this up. It's equally forthright when it comes to the 'language issue': Dutch-speakers fought hard to have their language recognised by the haughty francophones, and are wary of any attempt to 'reintroduce' French on Flemish soil.

More sinister than this, however, is the party's shameless assault on ethnic minority groups, in particular the Moroccan community, which established itself here under a materials-for-labour deal between the two countries' governments in the late 1950s. Older voters and those in the suburbs seem particularly keen on the 'kick 'em out' rhetoric. More surprisingly, the VB has its followers among the Chassidic Jewish community, who fear attacks by 'Arabs' (a somewhat ironic situation, given that some Flemings, seduced by Nazi separatist rhetoric, helped deport Jews during the Second World War). Equally bizarre is the gay VB vote, supposedly borne out of a fear of homophobic assaults on gay people by young Muslims. (Whether the VB's hardcore support is any more gay-friendly, we will hopefully never find out.)

Antwerp is an increasingly polarized city, a place where bikers proudly display Iron Cross wing mirrors, where there is a degree of ethnic tension, where a local cultural critic will suggest meeting in a 'left-wing' café to reveal his colours. But this only makes it more compelling. "Paradoxically," says Lanoye, "fascism is good for the arts, so long as it is not in power, but only threatening to get hold of public life. Everything becomes more confrontational."

After years of dismissing the VB as a bunch of nutters who would soon pass into oblivion, intellectuals and cultural figures now have to acknowledge, and even justify, its popularity. They'll point out that in a country where politicians are famed for their flexible approach to fiscal probity, it's easy for an untried party to claim it's the only 'clean' one – and they'll laugh about the hapless British hack who translated one of their slogans, "*Nuud afrekening*" ("Time to settle the account"), as "No Africans". They're also ready to back the much-admired socialist mayor, Patrick Janssens: Tom Barmans, frontman of the cult band dEUS, is planning a pre-election rally.

The municipal elections promise to be a tense stand-off, but there are signs that some Antwerpenaars are waking up to what lies ahead: an October 2005 poll recorded the first drop in VB support for 15 years. Whatever the outcome, these are exciting, edgy times for a city that has known plenty, and the need for political and social engagement may well have saved sometimes self-congratulatory Antwerp from sinking into the hermetic, homogenous world of the bijou weekend break.

Antwerp can be reached by air and rail. Most visitors will come via Brussels, either from the Eurostar terminal at Gare du Midi, from where there are frequent trains to Centraal station (as well as to Ghent), or from Brussels airport, which has a coach connection to Antwerp and rail links to Ghent. Deurne airport is 3 km from Antwerp city centre; Centraal station is a short walk from the old town. Antwerp is also on the international Thalys train network, with high-speed links to Paris, Amsterdam and Cologne. There are few car ferries from the UK to Belgium, but Calais is just across the border, and Belgium's extensive motorway network is great for getting from city to city.

Both Antwerp and Ghent are fairly compact, and their historic hearts can easily be explored on foot; there's also an excellent network of trams and buses. Most locals get around on two wheels, and Flanders is cycling heaven: few hills, lots of cycle lanes, motorists with respect.

Getting there

Air

VLM, T 020-7476 6677, www.flyvlm.com, is the only airline to fly direct from the UK to Antwerp's Deurne airport, 3 km southeast of the city centre (see Airport information, below). If you're travelling to Ghent by air, you'll have to go via Brussels.

From the UK and Europe VLM flies from London City direct to Antwerp **Deurne airport (ANR)**, several times a day; the journey time is one hour, with returns starting at less than £50/€75.

Brussels airport (BRU) is served by several airlines from the UK and Europe; from the UK, the main carriers are **BMI**, from Heathrow, Aberdeen, Belfast, Cork, Dublin, Durham, East Midlands, Edinburgh, Glasgow, Inverness, Leeds/Bradford, Luton, Manchester and Stornoway; and **SN Brussels**, from Gatwick, Heathrow, Birmingham, Bristol, Glasgow, Manchester and Newcastle. (SN operates a codeshare with British Airways.) Brussels-Heathrow takes 80 minutes; returns start at £80/€120 with both airlines.

Ryanair flies from Glasgow Prestwick, Dublin and Shannon to Brussels South (Charleroi), with returns from about £20/€30 – but be warned, it's a two-hour bus and train transfer to Antwerp, with a change in Brussels.

From North America There are no non-stop flights from North America to Antwerp, so the best option is to fly into Brussels. **American Airlines** flies from Chicago and New York (Newark and JFK); **Delta** flies from Atlanta and New York (Newark and JFK); **United** flies from San Francisco and Washington.

Airport information

Deurne airport (ANR) Antwerp's airport, **T** 03-285 6530, www.antwerpairport.be, is blissfully small, with a check-in time of just 15 minutes. You won't be lingering, but there's a basic

→ Airlines and travel agents

American Airlines (USA), **T** 1-800-433 7300, www.aa.com
BMI (UK), **T** 0870-607 0555, www.flybmi.com
Delta (USA), **T** 1-800-221 1212, www.delta.com
Ryanair (UK), **T** 0871-246 0000; (IRE), **T** 0818-3030307, www.ryanair.com
SN Brussels (UK), **T** 0870-735 2345, www.flysn.co.uk
United (USA), **T** 1-800-864 8331, www.united.com
VLM (UK), **T** 0871-666 5050, www.flyvlm.com

Travel websites
www.cheapflights.co.uk/com
www.cheaptickets.com
www.expedia.co.uk
www.lastminute.com
www.opodo.co.uk/com
www.orbitz.com
www.travelocity.com

restaurant. Bus 16 takes you to Central station (€1); a taxi costs about €20.

Brussels airport (BRU) Belgium's main airport, www.brusselsairport.be, has one terminal, and all the facilities you'd expect of an international airport. There's an hourly bus to Antwerp, stopping at De Keyserlei; the journey takes 50 minutes and costs €8 each way. For Ghent, take a train via Brussels North to Sint-Pieters station; the hour-long journey costs €7.50.

Brussels South Charleroi airport Charleroi airport is 46 km south of Brussels. To get to Antwerp or Ghent from here, take the bus to Midi station in Brussels, €10.50 each way (takes about an hour), then take the train (see below). Charleroi is a former military airport with a café, duty-free shops and newsagents; a new terminal is due to open in 2007.

Train

Eurostar, **T** 0870-518 6186, www.eurostar.com, has frequent services from London Waterloo to Brussels Midi station, with returns from £59/€90. The journey time is about 2½ hours, which should come down when the British high-speed link is completed. Note that from 2007, Eurostar services will depart from St Pancras station. There are persistent rumours that Eurostar plans a direct service to Antwerp, though the company insists that this is not the case. From Brussels, there are direct rail links to Antwerp and Ghent with **Belgian Railways** (SNCB/NMBS), **T** 02-528 2828, www.b-rail.be, and the transfer price is included in your Eurostar ticket. There are two fast trains an hour to Antwerp's Centraal station (about 45 mins) and to Ghent's Sint-Pieters station (28 mins), from which tram 1 takes you to the Korenmarkt.

If you're travelling to Antwerp from another European city, you'll arrive at Berchem station, which has frequent connections to Centraal station; alternatively, tram 8 passes near the station on its way to Groenplaats and the Zuid. Centraal station is being redeveloped to accommodate international services.

Coach

Eurolines, **T** 0870-514 3219, www.eurolines.com, runs direct services from London Victoria to Antwerp's Rooseveltplaats, 10 minutes away from the city centre; returns from £49/€72.

Ferry

Transeuropa Ferries, **T** 01843-595522, www.transeuropa ferries.com, has several crossings daily between Ramsgate and Ostend, a four-hour trip; from £42/€62 return for a car and up to nine passengers. **P&O Ferries**, **T** 0870-598 0333, www.poferries.com,

offers sailings from Hull to Zeebrugge; returns from £200/€300.
Superfast Ferries, T 0870-234 0870, www.superfast.com, has
overnight sailings from Rosyth to Zeebrugge; from £280/€416 for a
car and two passengers. From either port, you can reach Ghent and
Antwerp within an hour. Alternatively, the French ports of Dunkirk,
Boulogne and Calais are all accessible from Dover. **P&O**, T 0870-
598 0333, www.poferries.com, and **SeaFrance**, T 0870-571 1711,
www.seafrance.com, between them offer 50 daily ferry crossings
to Calais (90 mins). **Hoverspeed**, T 0870-240 8070, www.hover
speed.com, has 15 daily sailings (55 mins). **Norfolkline**, T 0870-
870 1020, www.norfolkline.com, sails 10 times a day to Dunkirk.
SpeedFerries, T 0870-220 0570, www.speedferries.com, sails five
times a day to Boulogne, a 50-minute crossing. Intense competition
on these routes has seen prices tumble, with car-and-passenger
returns available for £50/€75 or less in low season or via special
offers. Boulogne–Antwerp is a three-hour haul; knock off half an
hour for Calais and 45 minutes for Dunkirk. Boulogne–Ghent takes
about 2½ hours. Antwerp is also a stop on a new inland route offered
by **EasyCruise**, T 0906 292 2000, www.easycruise.com, which runs
from Brussels to Amsterdam between August and November; £13.33
per night for a two-berth cabin.

If you'd prefer not to sail, take the train through the Channel
Tunnel, emerging near Calais. **Eurotunnel**, T 0870-535 3535,
www.eurotunnel.com, has up to four services an hour; the
35-minute crossing starts at £98/€145 return.

Getting around

Public transport
Trams and **buses** in Flanders are run by **De Lijn**, www.delijn.be,
and the network is both comprehensive and efficient. A single
ticket (valid for one hour) costs €1, a day pass €3: they can be
bought from drivers or on station platforms. You should stamp the
ticket in one of the on-board machines. Both Antwerp and Ghent

are small enough to explore on foot: in Ghent, you probably won't use public transport at all; in Antwerp, the most useful lines are 8, which runs from Berchem station to Groenplaats, then down to the Zuid, and underground lines 3 and 15, which run from Centraal station to Groenplaats.

There are two **trains** an hour in each direction between Antwerpen-Centraal and Gent Sint-Pieters; the 50-minute journey costs €7.50 each way. In Ghent, the **Elektroboot**, www.elektroboot.org, is a free **boat** service between the Korenlei and the Gent-Zuid parking lot that runs from mid-April to October. The 20-minute ride, partly designed for shoppers, passes the Ketelvest, Recolettenlei, Ajuinlei and Predikherenlei.

Car

Competitive ferry prices make driving to Antwerp or Ghent an attractive proposition, but you won't need the car once you've arrived. The Antwerp ring has been entirely rebuilt over the past couple of years, leading to considerable disruption. The inner ring (the Leien) is also being rebuilt, which has restricted access to the historic centre. Ghent, meanwhile, has a 'mobility plan' that has made large parts of the city centre car-free. The E17 motorway connects Ghent and Antwerp, a 40-minute journey.

As in the rest of Europe, Belgians drive on the right, and priority is always given to vehicles coming from the right, no matter how big the road you're on. Strict speed controls are in operation: 30 kph in the vicinity of schools and in town centres, 50 kph in other built-up areas, 90 kph on open roads and 120 kph on the motorway. Front and rear seat belts are compulsory. The drink- driving limit is 0.25 mg of alcohol per litre of blood, compared to 0.4 mg in the UK.

Cycling

Almost everyone in Flanders has a bike, and cycle lanes are ubiquitous. Outside both Antwerp and Ghent, there are clearly signposted rural cycling routes, perfect for a day trip.

Travel essentials

→ Travel extras

Climate Flanders is on a latitude with southern England, and the climate is broadly similar, though Antwerp seems to attract more than its fair share of rain. The most clement time to visit is between May and September, when temperatures can reach the 30s, though the misty autumn has its admirers. Ghent is dead at the end of July and in the first half of August: ideal if you want cheap accommodation and the place to yourself, but catastrophic for night owls.

Health The health service in Belgium is one of Europe's finest. Visitors from the UK receive free treatment if they have a valid European Health Insurance Card, available free on application (**T** 0845-606 2030, www.ehic.org.uk), but it's still advisable to have private travel insurance. No vaccinations are required.

Money Belgium's currency is the euro. There are plenty of bureaux de change; or use an ATM. It's not hard to spend money in Antwerp, but it is possible to see the city on a shoestring: the minimum daily budget for food and accommodation is €35.

Safety Antwerp and Ghent are safe at all times of day or night, but beware of pickpockets in touristy areas, around railway stations and when leaving bars and clubs at night. The bigger hotels are open 24 hours, but it's best to give advance warning of a late arrival.

Taxi

You can pick up a taxi by phone (see below), by hailing a cab in the street or at one of Antwerp's many taxi ranks – the most useful ones are on Groenplaats, on the Grote Markt, at Centraal station, on Leopold de Waelplaats, outside De Roma (in Borgerhout), and on Dageraadplaats. For a complete list, visit www.aptu.be, the website of the **Antwerpse Provinciale Taxi Unie**. The minimum charge is €2.77, then €1.25-2 per kilometre. Prices double between 2200 and 0600. Be warned that Belgian cab drivers don't always have a comprehensive knowledge of their cities. To book a cab, try the following numbers: in Antwerp, **Metropole**, **T** 03-231 3131, or **Taxi Sinjoor**, **T** 03-830 4656. In Ghent, try **Taxi Gent** or **V-Tax**, **T** 09-222 2222/225 2525.

Walking
Both Antwerp and Ghent can be seen on foot, although the latter's cobbles can be unforgiving. In Antwerp, it takes 10 brisk minutes to walk from Centraal station to the Grote Markt, and half an hour or so to walk from Groenplaats to the Zuid or 't Eilandje; in Ghent, a stroll around the city centre takes about four hours.

Tours

Boat tours
Antwerp **Flandria**, Steenplein, **T** 03-231 3100, www.flandria boat.com, offers 50-minute river cruises (€7, children €5.50), 2½-hour tours of the commercial port (€11.50/€8) and three-hour candlelight dinner trips (€55).

Ghent **Gent Watertoerist**, Graslei 7, **T** 09-266 0522, www.gent-watertoerist.be, offers guided 35-minute (€5) and 90-minute (€9) tours of historic Ghent. These depart from the Graslei (Mar-Nov, daily 1000-1800, Nov-Mar, weekends only 1130-1430). **De Bootjes van Gent**, **T** 09-223 8853, www.debootjes vangent.be, offers 40- and 90-minute guided city tours (€5/€9), departing from the Korenlei (Easter-early Nov, daily 1000-1800; night tours on request).

Bus tours
Antwerp **Antwerpen Averechts**, Kronenburgstraat 34 (bus 1), **T** 03-248 1577, www.antwerpenaverechts.be. Offbeat tours of the city's neighbourhoods, including Borgerhout, in English on request. Booking essential. From €10 for two hours.

Diamond Bus, www.brussels-city-tours.com. Hop-on/hop-off double-decker city tours (€11, valid for 24 hours), starting at Centraal station, with headphone commentary in eight languages (Apr-Oct, daily 1030-1630; weekends only in winter 1030-1530).

Cycle tours
Antwerp Antwerp's tourist office (see p30) offers two-hour guided cycling tours of the historic centre, 't Eilandje, Sint-Andries and the Zuid. Reserve in person. (Jun-Aug, Mon, Wed and Fri; €10, including bike). **Antwerpen Averechts** (see Bus tours above) organizes themed bicycle tours to Middelheim, Cogels-Osylei, the Left Bank, the Jewish district and the city's Turkish neighbourhoods.

Tram, carriage and rickshaw tours
Antwerp Touristram, Easter-Oct, 1100-1700, weekends until 1600; Oct-Easter weekdays 1300-1600. A bone-shaking 35-minute guided tour (€4) from Groenplaats through the centre and up to the Rijnkaai, with commentary in English, French, German and Dutch. **Dames Carriage**, T 0475-746620 (mob). Easter-end Oct, 1200-1800; off season weekends only. A 10- or 20-minute tour of the city centre (€10/€19) in a horse-drawn carriage, departing from in front of the Town Hall. **Vervoort carriage**, T 03-353 8270. A 20-minute tour of the city centre (€19), departing from Den Engel, on the Grote Markt. Easter-Sep, from 1200. **Jut en Aer**, T 03-699 8520. Apr-Oct 1200-2000. A city tour in a pretty horse-drawn tram, sponsored by the Palm brewery. The 40-minute trip costs €5 and departs from the Grote Markt. **Ate Cars**, T 03-324 3451, www.riksha.bewoner.antwerpen.be. Jul-Sep, 1100-1800. A 30-minute guided rickshaw tour (€5), from the Grote Markt. For all of these tours, you can just turn up rather than booking in advance.

→ **Useful websites**

www.visitantwerpen.be	www.ticketantwerpen.be
www.antwerpen.be	www.festival.be
www.gent.be	www.gentsefeesten.be
www.diamonds.be	www.filmfestival.be
www.kaaien.be	www.beerpassion.com

Culture

www.cultuur.antwerpen.be
www.antwerpart.be
www.museum.antwerpen.be

Cycling

www.vakantiefietser.be
www.fietskar.be
www.kickbike.be

Ghent De Koetsen van Gent (Coaches of Ghent), **T** 09-227 6246. Apr-Nov 1000-1830. Horse-drawn carriage tours (€25 for the coach) of historic Ghent, departing from the cathedral.

Walking tours

Antwerp Antwerp's tourist office organizes two-hour weekend walks in the historic centre with an English-speaking guide (€5), departing 1100 from the office on the Grote Markt; daily in July and August. Reserve up to 30 minutes beforehand. They also have some themed walk brochures: history, Rubens, 't Eilandje, a Madonna statues walk (all €1.50); a fashion walk (€4), and '12 Adventures in Antwerp' (an excellent introduction to less familiar neighbourhoods, €3.50). **Antwerpen Averechts** (see Bus tours) offers alternative walking tours.

Ghent Association of Ghent Guides, **T** 09-233 0772, www.gidsenbond-gent.be. Straightforward city walks and themed tours on anything from pubs to human rights. **Guild of Town Criers**, **T** 09-220 4802, www.towncriers.be. Oh hear ye! Book a pub crawl with a town crier (minimum 10 people; €21 per person, including boat tour and drinks), or take a free Sunday-morning tour of the city's markets (departing from Kouter; 1030, May-Sep). **Vizit**, **T** 09-233 7689, www.vizit.be. Offbeat group tours with a culinary, industrial, literary or criminological theme, and tours for toddlers and children.

Tourist information

Antwerp tourist office, Grote Markt 13, **T** 03-232 0103, www.visitantwerpen.be. Mon-Sat 0900-1745, Sun 0900-1645. An excellent source of information about sights, events, exhibitions and cultural activities. You can also book accommodation and guides here. For cultural events, try **Prospekta**, Grote Markt 40, **T** 03-220 8111. Tue, Fri, 1000-1800, Sat 1200-1700. There's a smaller office on Koningin Astridplein, next to the zoo.

   Ghent tourist office, Botermarkt 17a, **T** 09-266 5232, www.visitgent.be, offers similar services to the Antwerp office. In addition, there's **USE-IT Gent**, Sint-Pietersnieuwstraat 21, **T** 09-324 3906, www.use-it.be, a 'tourist office for young people'. It's an invaluable, irreverent source of information for all travellers, especially those on a budget. It publishes maps and brochures on Ghent's sights, cultural activities, cheap eats and nightlife. The same goes for Antwerp, though there's no office there. In Ghent, pick up the **Museum Card** (€12.50 for three days), which offers free entry to 15 monuments and museums, including all those listed in this book. It's available from the participating institutions and the tourist office. On Sundays, 1000-1300, there are free guided tours of several museums, **T** 09-268 8460, directie.culture@gent.be.

   Week Up, www.weekup.be, is a free listings sheet showing what's on in both cities. The Dutch-language *Zone 03*, in Antwerp, and *Zone 09*, in Ghent, also offer comprehensive listings.

Historic centre

Somehow, Old Town doesn't feel like the right term for Antwerp's historic core. Wedged between the Scheldt and Sint-Katelijnevest, and narrowing to a triangle in the north, it has all the sights and sounds you'd expect from a late medieval metropolis: a slim-spired, soaring **cathedral***; an extravagant main square,* **Grote Markt***; the turreted* **Steen castle***, gilt gables, carillon peals and the ring of hoof on cobble. But there's something disorientating, too: the whole place has a slightly unmanicured look, there are dull and shabby stretches, and the sticky smell of waffles is perpetually on the breeze. In other words, this is a living city centre, based on the needs of the locals, not a tourist-thronged medieval theme park. And even the most workaday street has its share of hidden gems: on dreary Lange Nieuwstraat, you'll see stout baroque doors, a 'streaky bacon' Gothic chapel, and* **Sint-Jacobskerk***, the church where Rubens is buried. One of the joys of exploring is stumbling on a concealed courtyard or alley where there's nobody else to disturb your delight; and, thanks to the wiggly medieval street pattern, you can wander for hour upon hour, only to find that you have barely progressed from the first sight you set out to admire.*

▸ See Sleeping p123, Eating p140, Bars and clubs p163

◉ Sights

Groenplaats
Map 2, D5, p252

This windswept, slightly charmless square may seem an odd place to begin a tour of Antwerp's historic core, but it's the transport hub for the centre, and likely to be your first taste of the city proper. 'Green Square' was a cemetery in the 18th century, although all you'll find below ground level these days is a car park. The central cross was replaced by a **statue of Rubens**, Antwerp's most illustrious citizen. He stands, palette in hand, looking suitably proud of his achievements. The square's name is somewhat optimistic – grey would be more accurate – but there's a pleasing bustle and a remarkable concentration of bars. Groenplaats is dominated by the elaborate **Grand Bazar**, a former department store that's now the Antwerp Hilton, but your eye will continually be drawn to the spire of the nearby cathedral, a short stroll away.

★ **Onze-Lieve-Vrouwekathedraal (Cathedral of Our Lady)**
Handschoenmarkt, T 03-213 9940, www.dekathedraal.be. Weekdays 1000-1700, Sat until 1500, Sun 1300-1600. €2. Phone in advance for free cathedral tours with a volunteer guide. Map 2, C5, p252

No matter how many times you've seen it – from the Groenplaats, on postcards, on the front of glossy visitor guides, on the tourist office's homepage – nothing prepares you for the glory of this cathedral's spire, which soars at a neck-cricking angle over the cramped, cobbled Handschoenmarkt. Antwerpenaars are justly proud of what Sir Thomas More called "a masterpiece of art": 123 m of sleek, intricately carved stone, it's one of the finest Gothic structures in the low countries, and was, for centuries after its completion in 1521, the region's tallest building. What you don't see on the postcards, however, is the sad little stump right next to the spire, the city's abortive attempt to build a second tower. Though it gives the whole structure an asymmetrical feel, it also lends the façade a certain poignancy – a mirror, somehow, for the city's post-Reformation fall from grace.

The interior was certainly a casualty of religious conflict, looted by iconoclasts in the 16th century and by French revolutionary forces in the late 18th century. As a result, it's less breathtaking than the exterior leads you to expect – but it redeems itself by having kept hold of several spectacular Rubens paintings. The most famous, in the south transept, is *The Descent from the Cross*, in which Christ,

Inspiration in stone
The soaring spire of the Cathedral of Our Lady is a masterpiece of Flemish Gothic architecture.

▶ Return of the saint

Though it's now regarded as one of Rubens' finest achievements, *The Descent from the Cross* apparently dismayed his clients, the Guild of Arquebusiers. They had commissioned a portrait of their patron saint, Christopher, for their chapel in the cathedral, not a triptych depicting Jesus' death. Rubens, however, was constrained by an edict that only scenes from Christ's life could be shown in churches. His solution was typically cunning:

Christopher translates as "he who carries Christ", and this becomes a key theme in all three panels. In the main picture, St John carries His body; in the left-hand panel, Mary is pregnant, and thus carrying Christ; and in the right-hand painting, Simon holds the baby Jesus in the Temple. As a reminder of the original commission, St Christopher appears on one of the outer wings.

despite his deathly pallor, is still a source of light. Painted in 1614, it's clearly influenced by Rubens' eight-year stay in Italy, but amid the serious spiritual intent, there's a typically Flemish attention to material details: you can see the painter's delight in "the composition and the contrasts, in the portrayal of a sinewy body, in the hang of a dress, in the dignity of a bearded head," as the Dutch historian Pieter Geyl put it. A companion piece, The Elevation of the Cross (1610), full of typically muscular men, hangs in the north transept; The Assumption of the Virgin (1625) is on the high altar; and The Resurrection of Christ (1612) is in a side chapel in the choir.

The cathedral has strong links with England: the stained-glass window in St Anthony's chapel was a gift from Henry VII and Elizabeth of York in 1503, to celebrate a lucrative trade agreement with the Burgundian Duke Philip the Fair; and the virtuoso virginal player John Ball, author of *God Save the King*, became organist here after fleeing England in 1613. He claimed to have suffered religious persecution, but was in fact escaping charges of adultery.

Aficionados of religious architecture should buy *A Key to the Revelation of the Cathedral of Our Lady at Antwerp*, an excellent and often irreverent booklet by the art historian and priest Rudi Mannaerts. Otherwise just stroll around the cathedral, which, delightfully, butts right up against the bars and restaurants of beautiful **Blauwmoezelstraat**. Contact the tourist office if you want to visit the spire. It's a tiring trek up, but worth it for the views of the Grote Markt and sheer hugeness of the winding Scheldt. On a good day you can see the Atomium in Brussels.

● *There are four statues of the cathedral's builders on the right-hand side of the façade – except at weekends, when they're joined by a fifth flesh-and-blood member, one of several street-theatre artists who ply their trade (often slightly irritatingly) on this square.*

Vlaeykensgang
Entry at Oude Koornmarkt 16. Map 2, D4, p252

Southwest of the cathedral is a delightful alleyway of medieval houses. A slum in the 1960s, it was snapped up and lovingly restored by the antiques dealer Axel Vervoordt (see p95) and is now a mix of residences and restaurants. Its whitewashed appearance dates to the 19th century, when white chalk was thought to keep vermin at bay. Cholera outbreaks had previously claimed many citizens, among them Bruegel's son Jan, who worked with Rubens. Leave via Pelgrimstraat for a superb view of the cathedral spire.

Grote Markt
Map 2, C4, p252

Follow Oude Koornmarkt towards the river and you will suddenly spy the scrolling gables, leaded windows and golden statues of the guild houses on Antwerp's showpiece square. It's an impressive reminder of the wealth of the city in its 16th-century heyday, though it's more sprawling and less coherent than its counterpart in Brussels. (A good thing to point out if you want to wipe the smug smile off an Antwerpenaar's face.)

The city centre was battered by bombs and V-2 rockets during the two world wars, so it's not perhaps surprising that few of these Flemish Renaissance-style buildings, originally erected after a fire in 1576, are as old as they look. Sticklers for authenticity should focus on the third house from the left on the northern side: as the sculpted bows, suggest, it was the house of the Archers' Guild. The most imposing structure is the doughty Renaissance **Stadhuis** (Town Hall), built in 1564 and a perfect illustration of the post-Gothic enthusiasm for Italian discipline and harmony. The golden eagle on top indicates that, in the Middle Ages, Antwerp lay within the German empire.

In front of the Stadhuis, there's a dramatic, even gruesome statue of a man hurling a severed hand high into the air: if you've done your homework, you'll know that the man is **Silvius Brabo**, and that the hand once belonged to Druon Antigon. According to legend, the giant Druon Antigon settled on this stretch of the Scheldt, demanding a toll from any boats that passed through. If the captain was courageous enough to confront him, Antigon would slice off his hand in punishment. One day, inevitably, he met his match: a Roman soldier (Silvius Brabo) slew the giant, chopped off his hand and flung it into the river. Sculpted with relish by Jef Lambeaux in 1887, it's also a fountain, with water gushing gorily from the back of the hand, and the rocks at its base function as a handy climbing frame for children.

Volkskundemuseum

*Gildekamersstraat 2-6, **T** 03-220 8666. Tue-Sun 1000-1700.*
€2.5 (or free with ticket to the Etnografisch Museum, see p44).
Map 2, C4, p252

The low-tech but characterful Folk Museum (some captions in English) gives you a sense of daily life in the city until the 19th century. The eclectic ground-floor display includes old organs, shopfronts, a penny farthing, sedan chairs, a swan-shaped sleigh and paintings of pageants and peep shows, as well as puppets that pop out of coffins. To a soundtrack of cathedral bells, you'll discover that goose-riding was popular at inns and that "drink and games have always been an unbeatable combination".

Upstairs, meanwhile, you'll learn that citizens used to place an irreverent statue, 'Teun the Chicken Farmer', on the Eiermarkt to annoy the authorities, and that the rich could buy their way out of military service (which was abolished only in 1993). Other notable items include a magnificent doll's house with a copper kettle, a sinister school whip and a reconstructed Regency-style pharmacy with a model crocodile suspended from the ceiling.

Oude Beurs (Old Stock Exchange)
Map 2, B4, p252

North from the Grote Markt, follow Hofstraat (Rubens' father, a lawyer, lived at No 22), then cross Oude Beurs and turn right into the atmospheric, slightly crumbling courtyard of the **Old Stock Exchange**. Built in the late 15th century, when Antwerp was becoming a serious player on the European stage, it has the city's only surviving Gothic tower. On the day a ship was due, these enabled anxious merchants to see whether precious cargoes of Indian diamonds or Chinese silk had survived pirates and other hazards at sea. The building has no roof because the deals struck here were supposed to be transparent to God. As the city entered its golden age, with international merchants shifting their operations from the waning city of Bruges, the exchange soon outgrew itself and a larger one was built (see p47). The ground floor is used as office space by civil servants, but you hardly notice that as you stroll through the creeper-clad cloister in almost eerie silence.

Antwerp al fresco
Cafés and bars jostle for custom on Groenplaats.

Zirkstraat
Map 2, B5, p252

In the 16th and 17th centuries, the building on Zirkstraat that now
houses the El Valenciano delicatessen was the meeting place for
the Spanish community. Stoelstraat, north of Zirkstraat, is an
almost stiflingly narrow medieval street, its skinny houses seeming
to bend towards each other. The **Houten Gevel**, at no 11, is one

of the few surviving wooden houses in the city. As Antwerp grew, with citizens preferring to live within its walls (protected by the night-time curfew), lack of space became a problem. The only place to expand was upwards, so extra storeys were built, each protruding further into the street to take in maximum light.

Sint-Pauluskerk
*Veemarkt 14, **T** 03-232 3267. May-Sep, 1400-1700. Musical masses May-Sep, Sun 1030. Map 2, A5, p252*

"If you haven't seen St Paul's," says the church's brochure, "you haven't seen Antwerp." This may be overstating the case a little, but it's certainly one of the city's finest halls of worship, its late-Gothic façade belying the feast of uplifting baroque architecture within. The high white ceiling gives a real feeling of light and space, offsetting the black and white tiles, the marble columns, the gilt organ and the inevitable sculptures of cherubs and grapes. The collection of paintings is like a 'Who's Who' of Antwerp artists: Rubens, Van Dyck, Jordaens, Teniers, De Vos. Even the piped harpsichord music has a certain class.

On the way out, you pass a statue of Catherine of Siena, a Dominican saint who was reputedly anorexic and, perhaps not surprisingly, hallucinated during Communion. Outside, look out for the mock-up of **Mount Calvary**, erected rather haphazardly by two Dominican friars in the early 18th century. Baudelaire dismissed it as "ridiculous", but his opinion may count for little, as he was both a notorious Belgophobe and, at that time, in the advanced stages of syphilis. Note the pretty houses with glass-panelled windows on nearby **Lange Koerpoortstraat** (Nos 21-27).

! The word *'clochard'* ('tramp') comes from the curfew bells (*'cloches'*), which rang at 2200 every night. Only those with permits had the right to remain inside the city after this time.

Villa Tinto

Verversrui 17-19, T 016-490000, www.villatinto.com.
Map 2, off A6, p252

In typical Antwerp style, it's but a short step from the sacred to the profane. Northeast of Sint-Pauluskerk is the official red-light district, centred on the dark but neon-lit 'House of Pleasure'. Prostitution has long been rife in this seamen's city, but by the 1990s illegal brothels had made much of this area a no-go zone. Controversially, the city established a 'tolerance zone' in 2001, imposing stringent regulations – and tax – on brothel-owners, with the revenue used to fund a dedicated police unit. While illegal prostitution is still depressingly common, this initiative at least offers a degree of security to those working within the zone.

Villa Tinto itself is a high-tech affair, with a biometric ID system and panic buttons in each room. The designer, Arne Quinze (he's made furniture for Brad Pitt), worked in consultation with prostitutes to make the place as safe and comfortable as possible. You can even buy Villa Tinto T-shirts (and condoms, naturally).

Vleeshuis

Vleeshouwersstraat 3840, T 03-233 6404, museum.antwerpen.be/vleeshuis. Tue-Sun, 1000-1700. €2.50. Map 2, B4, p252

Heading south again on Vleeshouwersstraat, the Butchers' House is the best surviving example of Antwerp's 'streaky bacon' architecture, a striking effect achieved by using alternate layers of brick and sandstone. A lofty, castle-like structure, it was built several metres above sea level and dates back to 1501. As the name implies, it was home to the powerful Guild of Butchers and, rather gruesomely, to their abattoir and market, a spacious hall with a spectacular vaulted ceiling on the building's ground floor. For decades, this was a local-history museum but, with the vaunted arrival of the Museum aan de Stroom (see p90), it's being converted into a museum exploring the city's musical traditions from the Middle Ages onwards. Scheduled to open in autumn 2006, it will draw heavily on its unique collection of harpsichords fashioned by the Ruckers family, and promises not to be a 'conventional musical-instrument museum'.

Outside, look for the door leading to the city's smallest theatre, the **Polcinelle**, built in 1862 to supply soap opera-like entertainment for the local skippers and fish merchants. Just before you reach the riverside road, you can see surviving chunks of the 11th-century **city wall**.

Much of the area around the Vleeshuis was heavily bombed during the Second World War, and the remains of medieval houses and slums were replaced with a complex of red-brick social housing that respects the curving medieval street pattern. The old merchants' houses on nearby **Kaasstraat** offer a sense of what this area looked like in the 16th and 17th centuries.

Het Steen and Nationaal Scheepvartmuseum
*Steenplein 1, **T** 03-201 9340, museum.antwerpen.be/ scheepvaartmuseum. Tue-Sun, 1000-1700. €4. Map 2, B3, p252*

Antwerp's oldest secular structure, the castle can trace its origins to the ninth century, but this incarnation is mostly a mix of 13th- and 16th-century masonry. The fairy-tale turret is a 19th-century touch. Originally a fortress, the Steen was used as a prison and place of execution for several centuries. The painter Adriaan Brouwers, known for his ribald café scenes, often wound up here for being in debt, only to be bailed out by his influential friend Rubens. (For a price: Rubens ended up with 17 of Brouwers' paintings.) If the building seems a little isolated, that's because the surrounding houses were demolished in the 19th century, when the old curving quays were straightened.

The mocking figure, arms akimbo, on a pedestal outside is **Lange Wapper**, a devilish water spirit who could shrink or swell at the drop of the hat, scaring the living daylights out of drunks (one of the two penitent men in his shadow is clutching a bottle of genever).

Inside, the **National Maritime Museum** is an appealingly old-fashioned hotchpotch of pottery, ropes, tobacco boxes, model ships and paintings of dockers and mussel-fishers, as well as a scary-looking set of tattooing needles that helps explain why only real men used to have them. Among the many historical views of Antwerp, there's a fabulously detailed panorama from 1515, looking over from the left bank of the Scheldt and showing the medieval city in all its splendour. Downstairs, there is an impressive model of a passenger steamer, built in Liverpool for the Red Star Line, which carried passengers from Antwerp to New York between 1873 and 1935 (see p88).

Outside, there's a slightly random collection of supposedly historic boats in the elegant warehouses that stretch north along the river. If it's not too windswept, you might prefer to wander along the waterfront on an elevated walkway. At the far end, refreshment is on hand at the Noorderterras Café (see p143).

● *You'll notice that there are no bridges over the river. To find out how to reach the left bank, see p53.*

Suikerrui
*Etnografisch Museum: Suikerrui 19, **T** 03-220 8600, museum.antwerpen.be/etnografisch_museum. Tue-Sun 1000-1700. €4. Ruihuis: Suikerrui 21, **T** 03-232 0103, www.ruihuis.be. 3-hr underground tours in Dutch at 0930 and 1400. Advanced booking essential. Group tours in English on request. Map 2, C4, p252*

In the 19th century, several wealthy German merchants built elaborate houses south of the Grote Markt on 'Sugar Street' (ships used to carry sugar along this former waterway).

Thanks to Antwerp's status as a global trading hub (and, less happily, Leopold II's brutal stab at empire-building in the Belgian

Congo), the **Ethnographic Museum** can draw on a huge array of art and artefacts from far-flung parts. The bewildering richness and diversity of the collection – masks and statues from Africa, carved tribal poles from Irian Jaya, Native American headdresses, Indian Buddhas, Chinese ceramics, even a Maori canoe – more than make up for the slighty fusty air and the sparse English commentary.

Unlikely as it seems, the city's medieval sewer network (**Ruihuis**), was one of 2005's top tourist draws, with group tours booked up months in advance. Its success can partly be explained by its secondary function as a hiding place and escape route in troubled times, but it's also down to presentation: the party is decked out in full waterproofs and wellies, each member carrying a hand-cranked torch that whirrs like a dynamo. Though there are no 'sights' as such, wandering underneath the Grote Markt offers a certain frisson, and the brick vaulting is undeniably impressive (eminent Antwerp architects used to have dinner parties down here). It's dank and musty, and the smell is rather like a car park stairwell on a Sunday morning (alarmingly, perhaps, you get used to it). The tours are designed for large groups, but for €2 you can enter a small section of the sewers and have a sniff about.

Back on Suikerrui, you'll see **Grote Pieter Potstraat**, a narrow street heading south that bears the name of the 15th-century Dutch trader Pieter Pot, a kindly soul who distributed raisin bread to prisoners awaiting execution in the Steen. And on the way to the Grote Markt (still on Suikerrui), you'll pass a noble statue of a docker by the 19th-century sculptor Georges Minne. At the corner of Grote Markt, the **Anthony van Dyck ice-cream parlour** is named in honour of the artist's birthplace – you can glimpse a little of the original façade of the family home behind the roof.

! When you see a street name ending in '*rui*' (small river), '*vest*' (a man-made channel) or '*vliet*' (a small harbour used at high tide), you know you are walking on what used to be water. There are still 8 km of navigable waterways beneath the city.

Van Dyck's grandmother owned a cloth shop, which helps explain his ability vividly to depict textured fabrics.

Oude Koornmart and around
Map 2, C-D4, p252

On Oude Koornmart (the continuation of Suikerrui), you can see the Gothic façade of the city's first **Hansa House** (No 26), now being restored. **Hoogstraat** (High Street), to the south, is a bustling commercial thoroughfare, as it has been for centuries, and a handful of 16th-century houses are still visible. The house at No 3 (1578) marks the 16th-century limit of the city. In medieval times, there was a mixed 'bathhouse' (really a high-class brothel) on **Stoofstraat** (Stove Street). The **Sint-Julians Zwarte Panter Guesthouse** (Nos 70-74) offered three days' lodging to citizens setting off on a pilgrimage, hence its location on the edge of the city. (It's now an art gallery, with erratic opening times.)

★ Hendrik Conscienceplein
Map 2, C6, p252

East of Grote Markt, this stately, harmonious plaza, its cobbles prettily arranged to form little squares, was built by the Jesuits in Italianate style and is known as 'Little Rome'. It takes its name from the author of *The Lion of Flanders*, the first great Flemish novel. One of the city's loveliest squares, it is best approached via Blauwmoezelstraat, Kaasrui and picturesque Wijngaardstraat, with its restaurants and jewellers.

! In the 1960s, the artist Panamarenko blockaded the entrance to Hendrik Conscienceplein with hunks of ice in an effort to promote pedestrianization. The city authorities melted, and the square has been car-free ever since.

Sint-Carolus Borromeuskerk
*Hendrik Conscienceplein, **T** 03-231 3751, www.topa.be. Mon-Sat 1000-1230, 1400-1700; Sun for worship only, artists' mass 1130. Map 2, B7, p253*

Though the cherubs may be a little too kitsch, baroque doesn't have to be in bad taste, as this elaborate but never overwrought church bears witness. Built by the Jesuits between 1615 and 1621, it was dedicated to the order's founder, Ignatius Loyola, switching to a new saint, Charles Borromeo, when the Jesuit movement was suppressed in 1773.

Adorned on the outside with trumpeting angels, oysters and tumbling fruit, it was designed as a feast for the eyes, a sensory overload that led to it being called the 'marble temple'. Sadly, the building was ravaged by fire in 1718, destroying much of the interior decor and the 39 ceiling paintings by Rubens. The reconstruction was relatively sober, but the interior is still astonishingly opulent, with a floor of polished black and white tiles and a cream and gold colour scheme; the Mary chapel is particularly lavish. On the pulpit, the triumphant figure of a woman surrounded by angels, daggers and burning books, symbolizes the church destroying heretics. Ingeniously, the paintings behind the altar (Crowning of Mother Mary by Cornelius Schut, Erection of the Cross by Gerard Seghers, Our Lady of the Carmel by Gustave Wappers), rotate according to the religious calendar. Though Rubens' paintings are no more, you can still see his hand in the rakish design of the tower.

● *A plaque at the corner of Wijngaard and Wolstraat marks the red-brick house where painter Albrecht Dürer stayed in 1520.*

Handelsbeurs
Twaalfmaandenstraat. Map 2, D6, p252

Antwerp's second, highly elaborate stock exchange – the first of its kind in the world, the 'mother of all stock exchanges' in terms of its sheer size, but now defunct – is housed in this handsome Gothic structure, built in 1531, where thousands of foreign merchants conducted business, among them the English diplomat and banker Sir Thomas Gresham (of Law fame), who acted as financial agent to Elizabeth I. Demolished by fire in 1868, the building was painstakingly reconstructed, though the interior is closed to the public. (See also the old Oude Beurs stock exchange p39.)

Gresham lived in a Renaissance house nearby, at 43 Lange Nieuwstraat; just up the road, through an archway, is **Sint-Nickolas Godshuis**, a chapel in streaky-bacon style with a suntrap courtyard.

★ Rockoxhuis
*Keizerstraat 12, **T** 03-201 9250, www.rockoxhuis.be. Tue-Sun 1000-1700. €2.50. Map 2, B7-8, p253*

This rather down-at-heel street was home to some of the city's most influential figures, among them Nicolaas Rockox (1560-1640), longtime city mayor, head of the Guild of Arquebusiers and friend and patron of Rubens. At that time, Keizerstraat was a desirable area away from the smells, shouts and mayhem of the city centre.

The interior of No 12 is in Flemish Renaissance style, with gleaming floors in wood and tiles, sumptuous chests and splendid fireplaces. In these handsome surrounds, Rockox entertained a stream of artists and intellectuals. Among the many paintings are two tender depictions of the Madonna and Child, one by Quinten Metsijs, the other by Rubens. Don't miss Van Dyck's vivid study of two old men, Hans Bol's view of Antwerp, which shows a bluer-than-blue Scheldt cluttered with boats, or the 17th-century virginal decorated with tulips, foliage and berries. Do, however, resist the temptation to reach out for the fruit and vegetables in Joachim Beuckelaer's *Vegetable Sellers*, or the abundance of eels, lobsters and scuttling crabs in a painting of the fish market by Frans Snijders.

Splendid as the interior is, the real highlight is a lively 25-minute video (ask for the English version) that brings the noisy harbours and markets of 16th-century Antwerp vividly to life. In 1560, this was the biggest city north of the Alps, but the seeds of its decline were sown with the accession to the Spanish throne of the absolutist Philip II in 1555 – Antwerp was caught in the crossfire between Catholics and Protestants, and it paid a heavy price, its population halving by 1600. However, the rise of Rockox and Rubens, coinciding with the Counter-Reformation, led to an artistic and architectural revival, as wealthy families competed to fund churches and commission paintings. In this 'pearl of baroque in the north', the most successful artists became rich enough to buy palatial properties. But the deaths of both men in 1640 foreshadowed the city's final fall in 1648, when the Protestant Dutch insisted on closing the Scheldt as the price of peace with Spain. You can contemplate this sorry tale, against a backdrop of melancholic period music, in the quiet courtyard, with its loggia, vines, rosemary bushes and bay trees.

Sint-Jacobskerk

Lange Nieuwstraat 73-75, **T** *03-232 1032, www.topa.be.*
Apr-Oct daily 1400-1700, closed Sun. €2. Gregorian mass, Sun, 1000.
Map 2, D8, p253

It's hard to believe that this dark and chilly church was once *the* place to be buried, or that Ignatius Loyola, leader of the Jesuits, chose it as his residence when he stayed in the city. For all the marble, brass and swirling stone carvings, St Jacob's feels a little neglected. The main reason to visit is to see Rubens' tomb, which is tucked away in a small rear chapel. Surprisingly little fuss is made of it – there's a picture of the artist on a little easel, accompanied by a brief explanation in Dutch – but the tomb itself is sumptuous enough, with tumbling stone fruit and cherubs aplenty and, of course, one of the great man's works. A few chapels down, a glass case contains an attractive engraving of the Rubenshuis from 1684.

University district
Map 2, C7, p253

Antwerp's main university building is the **Hof van Liere** (Prinsstraat 13), a palatial place built in 1515-20 for the then burgomaster of Antwerp, given by the city to the all-important English wool-trading community in 1558, and hence known as the 'English House'. Dürer was much taken with it, declaring: "such a glorious building have I in the whole of Germany certainly never seen." You can visit during termtime, when the pretty, Oxbridge-like inner courtyard is open to all. Further east, the café-lined **Ossenmarkt** is one of the main student hang-outs.

Begijnhof
Rodestraat 39. Daily, 0800-1800. Free. Map 2, B10, p253

Most Flemish towns have *begijnhofs* – medieval housing complexes for communities of women who devoted themselves to prayer and charitable works, but who didn't care for the constraints of the convent – but this one is so hidden away that almost nobody visits it. More fool them: this is a perfect antidote to Antwerp's bustle, a neat complex of red-brick and whitewashed houses with overgrown cobbles and a pretty central garden.

Koninklijke Academie voor Schone Kunsten (Royal Academy of Fine Arts)
Mutsaertstraat 21. Map 2, B7, p253

Founded by the painter David Teniers the Younger in 1663, this is one of Europe's oldest art schools – and, as style swots will know, its fashion department is the alma mater of the Antwerp Six (see p56). Its most famous student, however, was Vincent Van Gogh, who moved to Antwerp in 1885 and spent a couple of months at the academy. In painting terms, it was a successful stay – "I find here the friction of ideas I want," he wrote – but he found the teaching stuffy and overly conventional and, after several disagreements with his tutors, dropped out to move to Paris. Sadly, he left all his Antwerp work in the city, possibly to pay off his landlord, and his depictions of the cathedral and the Steen have never been found.

Letterenhuis

*Minderbroedersraat 22, **T** 03-222 9321. Mon-Fri 0830-1630. €4, Fri free. Map 2, B6, p262*

This highly specialized museum is devoted to Flemish literature. The displays are sadly only in Dutch, but the friendly staff can provide enlightenment, and there are several witty touches: one author donated his delete button as a symbol of the anxieties that writers face in the computer age.

Stadswaag and around

Map 2, A7, p253

Northwest of the Hof van Liere, the Stadswaag (former weighing square), is a surprisingly pleasant space, lined with student bars and rarely visited by tourists. It had its bohemian heyday in the 1970s, when punks used to congregate here. Further north, across Paardenmarkt, stands the **Hessenhuis** (Falconrui 53, **T** 03-206 0350, museum.antwerpen.be/hessenhuis), a vast warehouse dating from the 1560s. Waggoners transporting merchandise between Antwerp and Germany could sleep and let their horses rest here: it now hosts temporary exhibitions (though none are currently scheduled); and, in the evenings, a gay bar (see p209).

Sint-Andries and the Latin Quarter

As you stroll past a seemingly endless stream of designer boutiques and modish brasseries, it's hard to believe that Sint-Andries was once so poor that it was a favourite setting for Zola-esque tales of desperation and poverty. Nowadays, you're more likely to find poor little rich girls checking out the latest graduates from the world-beating **Fashion Academy,** *which shares a handsome neoclassical building with the trendsetting fashion museum,* **MoMu. Nationalestraat** *and* **Lombardenvest** *are prime streets for fans of the Antwerp Six and their many successors;* **Kammenstraat** *is the place for street style, clubbing kit and piercings.*

If you're not a dedicated follower of fashion, head straight to the **Plantin-Moretus Museum,** *a remarkable Renaissance publishing house with ancient presses and rooms clad in ultra-luxurious leather. Further east, the* **Latin Quarter** *earned its name in the 19th century, thanks to its pungent mix of bohemians and brothels; like Sint-Andries, it's now considerably more refined, with elegant clothes shops, theatres and the restored* **Rubenshuis,** *a splendid Italianate mansion where the great man lived and worked.*

▸▸ *See Sleeping p126, Eating p145, Bars and clubs p166*

◉ Sights

Sint-Jansvliet
Map 2, D2, p252

This medieval harbour, one of several mini-wharfs dotted along the Scheldt, was filled in at the end of the 19th century. Its berths had become too small for the bigger cargo vessels, and it could only be used at high tide. Today, this *vliet* is a sociable square lined with restaurants and bars, while the basketball court in its centre is a magnet for the local 'yoof'. The best time to visit is on Sunday morning, when the charming flea market offers a chance to snap up vintage vinyl, obscure beer glasses and faded figurines of Laurel and Hardy. On the southwest corner of the square, the **Entrepôt du Congo** building served as a depot for goods shipped in from Belgium's African dominion.

★ Sint Anna voetgangerstunnel
Map 2, D2, p252

On the western edge of Sint-Jansvliet looms a yellow-brick building that resembles an art deco power station. In fact, it's the entrance to one of the world's longest underwater pedestrian passageways, a 572-m tunnel beneath the Scheldt. You can take the giant lift, which wheezes and whirrs like some kind of Jules Verne contraption, or the clanking wooden escalators down to the tunnel, which is clad in simple white ceramic tiles, with occasional markers to tell you how far you've got. Walking through is a strange, otherworldly experience, though you'll soon be brought down to earth if you don't keep an eye out for cyclists.

You emerge, via a twin of the Sint-Jansvliet entrance, on the city's left bank, the **Linkeroever**, a curious mixture of parkland and tower blocks. Antwerpenaars will tell you that the only reason to visit is for the view – and it's certainly a fine vista, taking in the cathedral spire, the Steen, Sint-Andries' bell tower and the hulking riverside hangars – but that's not entirely true, especially if you have children. There's a sprawling **nautical playground**, surrounded by barrels, buoys, anchors and propellers; and, in fine weather, Sint-Anneke beach (officially called **Sint-Annastrand**) is a prime sandcastle patch, though a dip in the Scheldt's polluted waters would not be a good idea.

★ Museum Plantin-Moretus

Vrijdagmarkt 22, T 03-221 1450, museum.antwerpen.be/plantin_moretus. Tue-Sun 1000-1700 (last entry at 1600). €6. Map 2, D3, p252

On three sides, Vrijdagmarkt is an unassuming little square that takes its name from its Friday-morning junk auction, an endearingly shambolic affair that, like so many things in this city, is best enjoyed from the comfort of a café terrace. The fourth side, however, is dominated by a handsome, fudge-toned 18th-century façade, behind which is one of Europe's most remarkable museums – the only museum, in fact, on UNESCO's World Heritage list, thanks to its "exhaustive evidence of the life and work of what was the most prolific printing and publishing house in Europe in the late 16th century".

The printworks was founded in 1576 by a Frenchman, Christophe Plantin, who moved to Antwerp in 1549 and swiftly established a thriving publishing business. He made his name with the Polyglot Bible, the first printed in five languages, including Hebrew, which boosted his Catholic credentials no end (in 1571, he became head printer to the Spanish Crown). Plantin, however, led something of a double life: he was a Calvinist, and printed several 'forbidden' texts, at great personal risk. In fact, in 1578, as the political tide turned, he became the official printer for the Dutch. At this point, he was running 16 presses and employed about 70 people, arranged in a loose trade union known as a 'chapel' (a term used by the NUJ to this day).

When Plantin died in 1589, the business passed to his son-in-law, Jan Moretus, and went from strength to strength. As well as the official Catholic Bible, the house printed dictionaries and books on the latest developments in science and architecture. Jan's son Balthasar was a close friend of Rubens – which explains the presence, in the upstairs living quarters, of 18 portraits by the artist – and the leading intellectuals of the day were regular visitors. The printworks survived until the 1870s, when it passed into the possession of the city.

The Renaissance complex is arranged, cloister-like, around a trim courtyard with neat balls of topiary and fragrant rose and lavender bushes. Visitors walk through atmospheric beamed rooms crammed with books and paintings, some lined with delightful gilt leather from Mechelen and Córdoba, to view proofreading desks and stout presses that date back to 1579. Remarkably, they still work, and are used to turn out copies of Plantin's sonnet, 'The Joys of this World'. These, for him, include a comfortable home, fine wine, a faithful wife, a debt- and quarrel-free life, few children and the ability to control one's "passions". Font fanatics will be thrilled to learn that the Plantin typeface originated here and that, even in this high-tech age, the museum's matchless collection of typefaces is often used as a benchmark for digital versions.

There are too many treasures to describe, but you mustn't miss the 1565 map of the city in room 23, which details every street, spire and harbour of Antwerp in its heyday. When you finally manage to drag yourself away, look up at the aeroplane-shaped weather vane on top of the neighbouring building, a reference to the V-1 bomb that destroyed much of the square during the Second World War.

Huis Draecke
Heilige Geeststraat 9. Map 2, D3, p252

Pop in for a peek at the courtyard of this 15th-century house, once inhabited by a merchant from Leipzig, who added the striking octagonal watchtower. The painter Jacob Jordaens, one of Rubens' most talented protégés, lived in the baroque mansion nearby, at Reyndersstraat 4.

► **Fashion: six of the best**

London Fashion Week, 1986: a group of young graduates from the Fine Arts Academy, instantly dubbed the 'Antwerp Six', stun the fashion world with a series of revolutionary shows and help transform their home city into a fashion powerhouse to rival Paris and Milan. It's hard to overstate their influence: until then, Belgian designers (among them Olivier Strelli, who designed clothes for the Rolling Stones) had always done their best to hide their untrendy origins.

Though Belgium appeared on the international fashion map almost overnight, this wasn't a spontaneous explosion of talent, but the result of both a calculated government effort to revitalize the ailing textile industry, and the fashion department's formidably challenging course. There's no denying the individual genius of the Six – Dries Van Noten, Ann Demeulemeester, Walter Van Beirendonck, Dirk Bikkembergs, Marina Yee and Dirk Van Saene – but they were merely the first of dozens of talented designers subsequently to emerge from the city. Now known as the Fashion Academy, their alma mater attracts students from around the world, though few manage to complete the rigorous, unchanging curriculum.

★ **MoMu**
*Nationalestraat 28, **T** 03-385 1638, www.momu.be.   Open only during exhibitions; Tue-Sun 1000-1800, Thu until 2100. €5.   Map 2, F4, p252*

The fashionably abbreviated Mode Museum is a shrine to the success of the city's designers, housed in an elegant neoclassical building, the ModeNatie, along with the **Flanders Fashion Institute** and the world-famous **Fashion Academy**. Rather than

It's democratic (tuition costs are low, and every student takes part in the end-of-year shows, which attract so much interest from fashion's movers and shakers that ticket sales easily cover the cost of the event), but it's also incredibly demanding. The lucky few who make it to the end, however, usually leave with a distinctive style and a deep-seated mistrust of licensing and branding deals; many choose to set up shop in the city, among them the German-born Stephan Schneider. He was one of eight students to have survived from an intake of 80. "That's normal," he says. "That's what it's like in the real world: not everyone makes it!" Schneider now has stores in Antwerp and Tokyo, as well as a concession at Selfridges in London. "Antwerpenaars," he says, "are passionate about fashion. Why else would Galliano and Westwood have opened shops in Antwerp?"

For Schneider, Antwerp has several attractions: radical, committed, unjaded designers; hard-working, proud manufacturers; relatively low rents; and a public that's prepared to splash out on high-quality clothes and good fabrics. If cool means not giving a damn, then Antwerp has it. "It's very laid-back," he says, "a fashionable place where what's 'in' doesn't actually matter."

a permanent display of clothes, this is a space for intelligently presented temporary exhibitions on a variety of themes: the influence of African dress and culture on western designers, for example, or a reinterpretation of traditional Russian garments by the contemporary design team AF Vandevorst.

On the ground floor, meanwhile, there's a permanent display introducing Antwerp's most prominent designers, as well as old corsets, fans and exquisite bits of lace; and the auditorium sometimes screens highlights of the academy's annual catwalk show, at which fledgling fashion gurus do their utmost to prove they can cut it with ever more weird and wonderful creations. Even if you couldn't give a fig for fashion, it's worth popping in to admire the atrium, a thoroughly modern mix of warm wood, glass and cool tiling, or browse at the bookshop, Copyright.

Nationalestraat and Kammenstraat
Map 2, E4/H3/F5, p252

Designer stores rub shoulders with cobblers, key-cutters and grocers on Nationalestraat, a sprawling street built in the 19th century to give the bourgeois residents of the new Zuid district an easy passage from the historic centre to their homes. To the east lies Kammenstraat, Antwerp's answer to Carnaby Street (then, not now), with a host of vintage and alternative fashion outlets and an unfeasible number of tattoo and piercing parlours.

Rather incongruously, the street is also home to the **Sint-Augustinuskerk** (Church of Saint Augustine, Kammenstraat 73, **T** 03-202 4660), a deconsecrated baroque edifice that now hosts early-music concerts. **Lombardenvest** was named after money-changers from Lombardy, who settled in the area; it's now best known for **Louis**, the first boutique to stock designs by the Antwerp Six, and still the best one-stop shop for the latest local talent.

Politietoren
Oudaan 5. Map 2, F5, p252

Also known as the Oudaan, the spiky concrete police HQ is unarguably one of the city's ugliest buildings, though as a statement of intent, it's certainly intimidating. Built between 1957 and 1967, it's a 12-storey slab of brutalist architecture at its most, well, brutal.

Sint-Andrieskerk

Sint-Andriesstraat, T 03-226 5253, www.topa.be. Jan-Dec, Mon, Wed, Fri 0900-1200; Apr-Oct daily 1400-1700. Free visit with a city guide, Sun 1500. Map 2, F3, p252

The area around this elegant Gothic church was once known as the 'parish of misery': most of the residents worked in the shipping trade, a precarious business thanks to the unpredictable nature of the Scheldt. *Natie* (guilds) were formed to provide aid to groups of workers such as dockers or weighers.

How things have changed: now surrounded by swish designer stores, St Andrew's is one of Europe's trendiest churches. It's run by the dashing Rudi Mannaerts, a cycling cleric who invited Ann Demeulemeester to design a dress for the church's Madonna statue. A notice outside the church describes God as "the DJ of all life", though, thankfully, they stop short of organizing raves for Jesus.

Named after the patron saint of the House of Burgundy, the church was founded by Augustinians in the early 16th century but never finished, because they were expelled from the city for sympathizing with Luther. It was the parish church of Rubens' first wife, Isabella Brandt, and the couple's children were baptized here. The pair should have married here, too, but Rubens favoured the more prestigious St Michael's Abbey, which sadly no longer exists. During the struggle for Belgian independence, the baroque tower served as a lookout post for keeping an eye on Dutch forces in their fortress on the Vlaamse and Waalse Kaais.

The pulpit shows Saint Andrew and his brother, Peter, whom Jesus invited to become 'fishers of men'; hence the fishing equipment and the delicious carvings of crabs, lobsters and plaice. Unexpectedly, there is a monument to Mary, Queen of Scots, dating from 1620, which reads "Seeking refuge in England in the year 1568 and taking up residence with her relative Elisabeth who reigned there, was then through the treachery of the senate and the envy of heretics beheaded in the cause of religion after 19 years of imprisonment, and accepted martyrdom in the year of our Lord 1587 at the age of 45." After Mary's execution in 1587, two of her ladies-in-waiting, Barbara Moubray and Elisabeth Curie, fled to Antwerp, where one had a relative.

Behind the church on Pastoor Visschersplein is a leafy red-brick complex of 1980s social housing offering views of the cathedral and St Andrew's. Off Korte Ridderstraat, you can spy a tiny 15th-century alleyway (accessed via the ivy-covered arch) that gives you some idea of what the old slums were like. Today, of course, such buildings are highly desirable. Korte Ridderstraat leads to Steenhouswersvest, where you will see many Madonna statues.

● *Take a short detour south to Rijke Beukelaarstraat, a mossy cobbled lane with step-gabled houses and pretty front gardens.*

Kloosterstraat
Map 2, F2/H2, p252

Now lined with cafés and congenial antiques shops, Kloosterstraat was originally the cloister wall of the 12th-century Abbey of St Michael, which explains its unusual straightness by medieval road-building standards. The abbey was a palatial domain, and the venue of choice for entertaining visiting VIPs; Rubens' mother was buried there. Sadly, it was wrecked during the French Revolution and the remains were destroyed by fire. A plaque in memory of the abbey is on the façade of the **Mercator-Orteliushuis** (Nos 11–17). This handsome house is wrongly named, as neither the map maestro Mercator nor the Antwerp geographer Abraham Ortelius actually lived here. The 'streaky bacon'-style mansion with

! The Virgin Mary is Antwerp's patron saint, which explains why there are upwards of 100 Madonna statues on street corners across town. Most date from the 18th and 19th centuries. The tourist office sells a 'Madonna Walk' brochure.

baroque additions is now a centre for archaeology and heritage. Slip in to see the statuary in the cobbled inner courtyard.

The rejuvenation of Kloosterstraat started in the 1980s and was sealed by the growing fashionability of the Zuid, into which it leads. It's a potterer's paradise, with a few sights to look out for. No 81 has an extraordinarily elaborate façade with carvings of fruit. Further down, there's a statue of Peter the Great, looking quite the dandy, with wavy hair and a dainty twirling moustache; the redoubtable Russian tsar visited Antwerp to learn about shipbuilding, and this monument was erected by the city's Russian community in 1998. The 16th-century **Heilig Huiske** (No 155) houses a café with a pretty terrace and garden.

Willem Leppelstraat was once a street of brothels; originally Leppelstraat (Spoon Street), it had the Dutch king's name added to help it overcome its dubious reputation. At No 10, 't Paardepoortje, an alleyway leads to a preserved section of the old slums, complete with outdoor toilets.

Huis van Roosmalen
Corner of Sint-Michielskaai and Goede Hoopstraat. Map 2, G1, p252

Kloosterstraat runs parallel to the waterfront, and is a prettier route to the Zuid than the windswept and slightly desolate quayside. Make a detour, however, for this postmodern masterpiece, designed by the Antwerp architect Bob van Reeth in 1985. Inspired by a 1927 Adolf Loos design for Josephine Baker, Van Reeth mixes nods to the city's maritime traditions – porthole windows, a funnel on the façade – with sleek jazz-age stylings, all in a racy zebra-stripe design.

The building played a key role in attracting investment to Antwerp's neglected wharves, as did Van Reeth's equally shipshape **Zuiderterras** (see Eating p147), a little further north.

Rubenshuis

*Wapper 9-11, **T** 03-201 1555, museum.antwerpen.be/rubenshuis. Tue-Sun, 1000-1700. €6 (joint ticket with the Mayer van den Bergh Museum). Map 2, E8, p253*

First, the bad news: the splendid mansion in which Rubens lived for 25 years is not entirely authentic. Though this "Italian island in a sea of Flemish brick" was the talk of the town on its completion, it was neglected for centuries after the artist's death, to the extent that it was practically in ruins by the end of the 19th century. During the Second World War, local architects persuaded the Nazi occupiers to let them rebuild and restore the house; it helped that Rubens was born in Germany. The monumental staircase, for example, dates from this period.

None of that, however, makes the place any less magnificent. As you enter, you'll see a traditional Flemish Renaissance house on your left and, on your right, an Italianate house with loggias, an eloquent reminder that Rubens was inspired by Italian architecture as well as art. In fine weather, it is tempting to head straight for the garden, but you'll learn far more if you start inside. The excellent audio-tour (available in English) allows you to select in-depth information about Rubens' marriages, his work as a diplomat and his love of a good party.

In the kitchen, with its Gothic fireplace and shiny copper pots, we hear that *soirées chez* Rubens often degenerated into binge-drinking, though the artist himself always managed to stay sober. Upstairs, you can see the room where Rubens died (1640) after an attack of gout, and portraits of his first wife, Isabella Brandt, and second, much younger wife, Hélène Fourment (she was 16 when they married). When Isabella died of the plague, Rubens talked of his "great loss", adding that the "only remedy is oblivion". Marrying Hélène, who served as a model for many of her husband's mythological paintings, evidently perked him up a bit. The bedroom, with a pretty terracotta floor, is hung with pastoral

Adam and Eve in Paradise

This early work by Rubens was painted before the trip to Italy that had such a profound effect on his artistic techniques.

landscapes by Jan 'Velvet' Brueghel (1568-1625), the finest flower painter of his day, and houses an oak and ebony writing chest.

In the living room, you can see portraits of the painter's grandparents and learn how his father, a lawyer, fled Antwerp because he was sympathetic to Protestantism. His mother took the 12-year-old Rubens back to Antwerp following his father's death. This goes some way towards explaining Rubens' determination to help bring peace to his war-ravaged homeland. The ease with which he mixed in high circles saw him broker a 12-year truce between Catholic Spain and Protestant England. He was knighted by Charles I and, ever the pragmatist, won important commissions from both royal houses.

Downstairs, you can visit the intimate antechamber, adorned with sumptuous Córdoba leather panelling, and the Great Studio, with its tall, Italianate windows. This was the heart of Rubens' "medium-sized business", where the artist and his army of assistants worked on canvas after colossal canvas. How much Rubens himself was involved in the process depended on the fee – he would often establish the outline, then return at the end to add the final flourish – but as his employees included Van Dyck and Jacob Jordaens, even the more parsimonious purchaser was unlikely to feel short-changed.

The paintings that now line this room reveal the extent to which Rubens' Italian trip (1600-1608) changed his approach: at first glance, you may prefer his solidly Flemish *Adam and Eve* to the swirly, curly, chubby-cheruby *Annunciation*. Look closely, however, and there's a new energy to his work, with invigorating contrasts between light and dark.

! Rubens' garden was converted into a riding school by exiled English royalists in the 1650s; the future Charles II stayed here for a few days. The lady of the house, Margaret Cavendish, described the locals as "the civilest and best-behaved people that ever I saw".

End your visit in the garden, which appears in several Rubens paintings and was recreated using the artist's botanical books and diagrams. It is easy to imagine Rubens strolling with intellectuals, artists and political figures, proudly pointing out a potato plant from the New World, a rare tulip or an orange or fig tree.

Meir
Map 2, E8, p253

This is Antwerp's answer to Oxford Street: at road level, it's a dismaying string of could-be-anywhere chains, but the buildings themselves are frequently splendid, an ensemble of florid neo-baroque buildings that reflect the mood of the mid-19th century, when the reopening of the Scheldt revitalized Antwerp's fortunes.

The station end is particularly impressive, framed by two giant domed structures, embellished with pillars, scrolls and statues. Look out also for the rococo buildings at No 85 and No 50, and take a detour down Kolveniersstraat to see the courtyard of the arquebusiers' guild house, the **Kolveniershof**.

Boerentoren
Meirbrug. Map 2, D6, p252

The 'Farmers' Tower' was Europe's first significant skyscraper, 87.5 m high. Built for the Antwerp Bank Association (1929-32), it owes its name to the fact that the Belgian Farmers' Union had a big share in the bank; it's now owned by the Belgian bank KBC. It's an attractive art deco tower that glows prettily pink come sunset, but reveals how much catching up European architects had to do: the Chrysler and Empire State buildings were both constructed in 1930.

★ Museum Mayer van den Bergh
*Lange Gasthuisstraat 19, **T** 03-232 4237, museum.antwerpen.be/*
mayervandenbergh. Tue-Sun, 1000-1700. €4, joint ticket with
Rubenshuis. Map 2, F6, p252

This gem of a museum contains a dazzling array of paintings,
statuary, tapestries and medieval missals assembled by the
19th-century collector Fritz Mayer van den Bergh, one of many
bourgeois Germans who lived in Antwerp (until the outbreak of
the First World War), and famous for reigniting interest in Pieter
Bruegel the Elder (1525-1569). Following his death, his mother
created this museum in a purpose-built neo-Gothic building.

   The eclectic nature of Fritz's taste soon becomes apparent:
he collected 12th-century religious statues from Champagne,
illuminated manuscripts, a medieval altarpiece from Spoleto,
tapestries from Brussels, even a Roman sarcophagus from the
second century. Highlights on the ground floor include a
16th-century painting of a blue-tinged winter landscape, in which
skaters slip and slide (Christoffel van den Berghe); Cornelis Ketel's
double portrait of a gorgeously dressed brother and sister, looking
watchful and mature; an anonymous painting of Antwerp's fish
market, circa 1600, with views of city and port; and a Crucifixion
triptych by Quinten Matsys.

   Upstairs, room 6 contains some of the museum's most
valuable treasures, among them a moving early 14th-century
sculpture of St John resting his head on Jesus' chest, by Master
Heinrich of Konstanz, and two small but stunningly delicate
panels of a 14th-century polyptych, showing the Nativity and
the Resurrection. Pieter Aertsen's 16th-century *Peasants by the
Hearth* shows a thoroughly Flemish sight: the remains of a feast,
with mussel shells scattered across the floor.

   Centre stage, however, must be given to Mad Meg, Pieter Bruegel
the Elder's nightmarish, hell-red painting of an angry old woman on
the rampage, against a backdrop of people fighting, a fish eating a

man and a gallery of grotesque faces and weird beasts. Influenced by Hieronymus Bosch, it has undeniable power, conveying madness, brutality and havoc, although experts are still debating what it really means. The standard line is that it is an allegory of madness, which in the 16th century denoted frenzy, anger, gluttony, lust and avarice; some see it as a critique of Spanish rule, others as a spot of unabashed misogyny. Canny Fritz snapped up this masterpiece for next to nothing at an auction in Cologne, sparking a rush of interest in an artist best known for his scenes of peasant life: Twelve Proverbs, in the same room, is a delightfully witty example.

Maagdenhuis
*Lange Gasthuisstraat 33, **T** 03-223 5620.   Mon-Fri 1000-1700, weekends 1300-1700, closed Tue. €2.50. Map 2, G6, p252*

This brick-and-sandstone building, which served as a girls' orphanage between 1552 and the late 19th century, now houses the art collection of the city's social welfare department. Many of the objects on display are poignant illustrations of the plight of the poor, most affectingly the tokens impoverished mothers gave their children when abandoning them, in the hope that they might one day be reunited. The beautiful polychrome bowls used by the children are precursors of Delft pottery.

As for the paintings, the highlight is Anthony Van Dyck's vast, dynamic *Christ on the Cross*, unmissable in all respects. The darkness shrouding Christ's face is in stark contrast to the sumptuous play of light on the surrounding costumes. There are several fine portraits, too, including an orphan girl by Cornelius de Vos, and a rather fierce-looking portrait of Elisabeth Hynderick, wife of the influential urban planner Gillebert van Schoonbeke, by Frans Floris. In an anonymous depiction of *The Last Judgement* (circa 1500), the capital sins are, inevitably, much more eye-catching than the works of mercy.

Centrum 't Elzenveld
Lange Gasthuisstraat 45. See Sleeping, p126. Map 2, G6, p252.

Primarily a conference centre, the 'Elysian Fields' does its best to live up to the billing. The tranquil complex houses the medieval St Elisabeth Hospital, one of the city's oldest buildings, and a 15th-century chapel, a delightful venue for classical concerts. In the courtyard are two ghosts, sculpted by Albert Szukalski, a potential night-time fright for drunken delegates. A modern hospital now stands next to the old, adjacent to the city's **Botanical Gardens** (Leopoldstraat), which were originally created as a herb garden for the medieval hospital. This is a modest, peaceful place, an oasis of calm splashed with colourful seasonal flowers and blossom, and with several benches for resting weary feet.

Bourlaschouwburg
Komedieplaats 18. Map 2, F7, p253.

The stately dome of the **Bourla Theater** was built by Pierre Bruno Bourla in the 1830s to cater for the dramatic needs of the city's French-speaking bourgeoisie. The Jesuits opened the first theatre in this neighbourhood in the 18th century, but they were soon crowded out by artists, writers and libertines, earning the area its 'Latin Quarter' tag. In the 1980s, real-estate developers wanted to demolish the theatre (it had closed for fire and safety reasons) and replace it with a car park; thankfully, the proposal was rejected and a restoration programme began. The building is now home to the city's No 1 theatre company, Het Toneelhuis (see p186); if your Dutch isn't up to scratch, the main draw here is the first-floor café, **De Foyer**, with its remarkable rotunda.

Diamond and Jewish districts

*When you arrive at the gloriously grandiose **Centraal station**, its vast arrivals hall dripping with gilt and marble, you'll be left wondering whether the rest of Antwerp can possibly be like this. Which only adds to the sense of bewilderment as you leave the station to find yourself on the blighted building site that is Koningin Astridplein, or amid the tacky jewellery shops on Pelikaanstraat. Even the elegant buildings of the Meir, route one to the historic centre, now house humdrum high-street chains.*

*First appearances, however, are deceptive. At the heart of this area, which sprawls away southeast of the station, is the diamond-dealing capital of the world, a secretive, security-conscious but strangely compelling string of streets where Indians, Africans, Chinese, Jews and Russians seal deals with the traditional handshake of trust and the Yiddish word "mazal". The surrounding neighbourhood, the **Jootsewijk**, is one of Europe's biggest Orthodox Jewish communities, known as the 'Jerusalem of the north'. Men with broad black hats, black coats and long, curling payos (ringlets) hurry about their business, apparently oblivious to the Gentiles around them. Even unlovely Astridplein is worth revisiting: for one of Europe's oldest **zoos**, with a faux-Egyptian elephant house among its spectacular architectural treasures; for the **Diamond Museum**, where you can learn exactly why the much-prized stones are a girl's best friend; and for the child-friendly **Aquatopia**, where you can be sure of finding Nemo.*

▸▸ *See Sleeping p127, Eating p149, Bars and clubs p168*

!
• The word 'carat' comes from Greek, meaning 'fruit of the Carob tree'. The tree's seed pods weigh approximately 2 g and so were adopted to assess the weight of various precious stones.

Sights

Station Antwerpen-Centraal
Map 2, E12, p253

There are few more uplifting ways to arrive in a city than to step off a train at Antwerp's central station. Built in 1905, on the orders of Belgium's megalomaniacal monarch, Leopold II, it's a riot of marble, mosaic, glass and wine-red wrought iron, with a vast fan-shaped window – lovely as a peacock's tail – loggias, columns and gilding. The main hall is on cathedral scale, with even the hustle and bustle deadened to a whisper by the sheer height of the ceiling.

Catch your breath on the monumental staircase, because the next stop couldn't be more different: take a left and you're plunged into **Pelikaanstraat**, parallel to the railway and awash with tacky jewellery shops – or shacks, to be precise – with names like 'Mr Diamant' and 'Golden Hand', selling chunky signet rings engraved with a € sign or jewel-encrusted crucifixes, all with pink price tags offering improbable discounts. If you've come to buy a diamond, move swiftly on; otherwise, this slightly seedy stretch holds a somewhat grim fascination.

Diamond district
Map 2, F11, p253

Pelikaanstraat may promise discount diamonds, but the serious stones are bought and sold behind closed doors in the small concentration of office blocks, glass and concrete between the station and the Stadspark. It's strictly trade only – diamond dealers are, not unreasonably, a secretive bunch – but it's worth wandering through to sample the atmosphere during working hours; otherwise, it's eerily deserted. This was a rural area until the erection of the station, hence street names like **Hoveniersstraat**

▶ Ice, ice, baby

Two-thirds of the world's raw diamonds, and half its polished ones, pass through Antwerp, where they are cut, set in jewellery or resold. The Antwerp cut has long been an international benchmark of quality, though it appears to have originated in Bruges, where Lodewyk van Bercken devised a unique polishing method involving diamond dust and olive oil. The diamond business moved to Antwerp in the late 15th century.

If you want to see polishers at work, you can pay a visit to the **Krochmal &** Lieber workshops located at Lange Herentalsestraat 29, **T** 03-233 2169, www.krochmal-lieber. com). The **Diamond High Council** (HRD) offers tours of

the diamond district (Hoveniersstraat 22, **T** 03-222 0511, www.diamonds.be, 1000-1200, €50; take passport).

If you are planning to buy a diamond, the question you should be asking is: how did it get here? The trade in 'blood diamonds' has helped fund numerous global conflicts, notably in mineral-rich African states such as Sierra Leone, and to buy one of these stones is effectively to condone mass murder. Antwerp's Diamond High Council (HRD) has imposed regulations on the sale of diamonds, insisting on government certification and traceability; look out for the ADJA (Antwerp Diamond Jewellers Association) logo, and ask for an HRD certificate.

(Gardeners' Street); now the standout sight is the pretty Portuguese **synagogue** (1913), which was bombed by Islamic extremists in 1981 (as noted on the memorial plaque). Since then, and even more so since 9/11, security has been stepped up, so you'll see plenty of guards and CCTV cameras.

Diamondland

Appelmansstraat 33A, T 03-229 2990, www.diamondland.be.
Mon-Sat 0930-1730, Sun 1000-1700 in summer. Map 2, E11, p253

In this surprisingly unglamorous showroom-cum-museum, you can watch polishers and cutters at work (from behind glass), learn about the processing of diamonds or snap up a sparkler and have it set while you wait. It is extremely popular with the newly engaged.
● *The Antwerp Diamond City Walk brochure, available for €1.50 at the tourist office and the Diamond Museum, details four walks with a girl's-best-friend theme.*

Koningin Astridplein

Map 2, D12, p253

This should be one of the city's showpiece squares, with the station at one end and several cultural and tourist-heavy attractions, but instead it has the air of a long-deserted building site. It's been this way for years: though plans are in place to revamp it, financial issues had put the project on hold at the time of writing. (Tantalizingly, you can scan billboards advertising the leafy, pedestrianized square-that-may-be while choking on dust and traffic fumes.) Facing the station is the **Astrid Park Plaza**, a monumental hotel whose playful postmodern interpretation of Antwerp's medieval buildings gets more stick than it perhaps deserves.

Diamant Museum

Koningin Astridplein 19-23, T 03-202 4890,
www.diamantmuseum.be. Summer daily 1000-1800 (closed Mon morning), winter until 1700. €6, Fri free. Map 2, F11, p253

Here you can learn about the origin, mining and peculiar properties of the world's most precious stone, beginning with the famous '4 Cs' (clarity, colour, carat and cut). A slightly puzzling interactive approach allows you to choose a 'character', such as a goddess or an alchemist – not really a tough choice – and the headphones trigger commentary for the exhibits, which you may be able to hear over the surrounding sound effects.

Indulge your thirst for knowledge by learning why diamonds are the hardest substance known to man (it's their symmetrical atomic structure), that they are useful insulators of electricity, and that they are called 'ice' because they rob the body of warmth when touched. Or allow your inner princess to gawp at four centuries' worth of the finest stones, including art deco items from Paris, and necklaces in which diamonds are set with coral, jade or lapis lazuli.

Antwerp zoo

*Koningin Astridplein 26, **T** 03-202 4540,*
www.zooantwerpen.be. Nov-Feb 1000-1645; Mar-Apr and Oct
1000-1730; May-Jun and Sep 1000-1800; Jul-Aug 1000-1900. €15,
children aged 3-11 €9.90. Map 1, D7, p251

Founded in 1843, this is one of Europe's oldest zoos – and in some enclosures, especially the depressingly pokey bird cages, it really feels that way. But that's true of many city zoos, and its status as a breeding centre for okapis, and the development of a more spacious wildlife reserve at Planckendael, near Mechelen (see p214), indicate a serious commitment to the welfare of the animals. With lions, tigers, elephants, rhinos, gorillas, baboons, giraffes, chimps and a sealion show among the attractions, children are sure to leave feeling happy; zoo-hardened grown-ups may be more impressed by the astounding period architecture, especially the Egyptian temple elephant house, complete with fake hieroglyphs.

Aquatopia

*Koningin Astridplein 7, **T** 03-205 0740, www.aquatopia.be. Daily 1000-1800. €11.45, weekend €12.45, children 4-12 €8/€9, family tickets available. Map 2, D12, p253*

"Look, it's Nemo, it's Nemo!" The Disneyfication of the oceans continues apace at Antwerp's child-friendly aquarium, where a whole tank of clownfish keeps younger children agog for hours. Elsewhere, there's lots of interaction, plenty of high-tech gimmickry – you can use a piranha cam to zoom in on the fearsome fish – and much genuflecting at the altar of ecofriendliness, but a puzzling absence of show-stopping moments. The shark tunnel, trumpeted rather crassly with an escalator descending into a great white's mouth (and the music from *Jaws*) turns out to house nothing scary enough to frighten the average turbot.

Stadspark

Rubenslei. Map 2, H10, p253

It's a little fatuous to call Antwerp the 'Milan of the North', but it shares with its Italian cousin a shortage of appealing green spaces. The best option in central Antwerp is this sprawling park, built on a 16th-century stronghold. The playground is frequented by families from the nearby Jewish district, and there are pretty water gardens; the highlight, though, is the Cinderella-florid bridge over the pond, a delightful place to offer that newly purchased diamond ring…

Design Center De Winkelhaak

*Lange Winkelhaakstraat 26, **T** 03-727 1030, www.winkelhaak.be. Mon-Fri 0900-1800. Free. Map 1, C7, p251*

This showcase for Flemish design, with studios for local talents, was built as part of a recent effort to breathe new life into a once downtrodden area. The floor-to-ceiling glass façades of the building recall the windows in which the local prostitutes were once on display. All you can pick up here, though, is a useful leaflet detailing an architecture tour. At the end of the street are some increasingly desirable city cottages in quiet cul-de-sacs.

Chinatown
Van Wesenbekestraat. Map 2, C12, p253

This is essentially just one street, with stone lions marking both ends. Chinese New Year is celebrated here, though partygoers have to dodge trams as they dance.

De Coninckplein
Map 2, C12, p253

The heart of an African neighbourhood, this square's main claim to fame used to be its drug addicts. It's now home to **Permeke**, a fabulous new library with a green-glass café and city information point, which has done much to boost the area's reputation. Non-residents can join for just €7.50 per year, which includes unlimited internet access.

Sint-Jansplein
Map 2, A11, p253

This is the heart of the city's Portuguese community, with cafés and restaurants aplenty; more recently, Polish shops have sprung up here. Look out for the Panamarenko statue of Pepto Bismo, a man with a magnificently mad flying machine.

▶ Jerusalem of the north

The first Jews in Antwerp arrived in the Middle Ages, fleeing persecution in Spain, Portugal and northwest Africa. The next influx of immigration, from France, Holland and Germany, took place in the 18th and 19th centuries; then, towards the end of the latter century, Jews came from eastern Europe, primarily refugees from the pogroms. Many found work in the diamond industry.

The 1930s saw another influx, this time from Hitler's Germany: some boarded Red Star Line ships to New York; others stayed, only to be deported by the Nazis, despite the help of the Church in sheltering many Jews. The 25,000-strong Jewish community had shrunk to just 800 by the end of the war; today, however, it numbers about 15,000.

The most visible members of Antwerp's Jewish community are the Chassidic Jews, who adhere strictly to the Torah and to Jewish law, with its detailed codes of behaviour. Heads are covered as a mark of respect for God (the men often wear more formal fur hats on the Sabbath) and out of modesty (women cover their heads once married, some even shaving them and wearing wigs); others wear a beret-like hat called a snood. Men and women generally do not shake hands or touch each other unless married. Similarly, a Chassidic man tends to avoid looking directly into the eyes of any woman other than his wife. From a young age, boys have skullcaps and shaven heads with curly ringlets. There are many Chassidic communities, each with its own synagogues and prayer houses. And, if you eat in a Yiddish restaurant, you may see men pausing from their meal to fervently pray.

Antwerp University has an Institute for Jewish Studies, opened in 2001. For details of Sabbath restrictions, visit www.ou.org/chagim/shabbat/thirtynine.htm.

Het Zuid

If a lifestyle mag were allowed to style a city, this is how it would look: a string of supercool bars and cafés, design shops offering high-concept homeware and deconstructed dresses, bright young things flitting from terrace to terrace, their only care the placement of their vintage sunglasses. Welcome to 'the South', an almost overly successful example of the power of urban regeneration.

Based around two filled-in quays, the Vlaamse Kaai and the Waalse Kaai, 'the South' is a succession of circular plazas with radiating streets. It's often described as 'Little Paris' (picking up on this theme, the monthly art market on Lambermontplaats is called 'Lambermontmartre'), but it hasn't acquired its big sister's notorious attitude. In any case, the art nouveau flourishes and ceramic tiles of the neighbourhood's handsomely restored town houses are unmistakably Belgian.

You could spend days here just people-watching, but there's plenty to do besides: the **Fine Arts Museum** holds a comprehensive collection of works by Flemish and Belgian masters; **Muhka** is a white-walled wonderland for fans of contemporary art; and the **FotoMuseum** offers top-drawer temporary shows. And, for every poseur's paradise, there's a deliberately down-at-heel drinkers' dive where more bohemian spirits will feel right at home.

▸▸ *See Sleeping p128, Eating p149, Bars and clubs p170*

Sights

Volkstraat
Map 1, F2, p250

As you'll guess from the interiors shops, delicatessens and chichi cafés, 'People's Street' links the fashion district and the Zuid. Its architectural highlight is **No 40**, a triumph of Jugendstil architecture adorned with graffiti motifs and crowned by an ornate half-oval window. Built as a meeting place and co-operative bakery for the Liberal party in 1893, it is now a Rudolf Steiner School.

Make time for a couple of detours: the **Institute for Tropical Medicine**, at Kronenburgstraat 43, is an intriguing, monumental mix of classicism and art deco that dates from 1924; while star-shaped **Marnixplaats** has an imposing statue of Poseidon at its centre, celebrating the removal of restrictions on the Scheldt.

★ Koninklijk Museum voor Schone Kunsten (Royal Museum of Fine Arts)

Leopold de Waelplaats, T 03-238 7809, www.museum. antwerpen.be/kmska. Tue-Sat 1000-1700, Sun -1800. €6. Tram 8. Map 1, F2, p250

The Fine Arts Museum, a grandiose neoclassical structure, dominates the vast Leopold de Waelplaats in the way that only a temple of culture can. Happily, it lives up to its billing, with the city's most wide-ranging collection of masterpieces both medieval and modern: the list below is only a whistle-stop tour.

Pausing to admire the mosaic floors and marble balustrades on the monumental staircase, head upstairs to **Room Q**, dedicated to medieval masters. You'll find a gorgeous golden Gabriel, one of four panels by the Sienese artist Simone Martini; two works by Jan van Eyck, including a splendid sketch of St Barbara, in which the tower under construction echoes Antwerp's cathedral; a typically restrained and moving Crucifixion triptych by Rogier van der Weyden, whose portrait of the nobleman Philippe de Croy at prayer has astonishing poise and piety. Next door, in **Room S**, you'll see a bizarrely garish *Madonna and Child* by Jean Fouquet; its ivory-skinned Mary and red and blue cherubs are more 1960s bad acid trip than 15th-century devotional.

Peep into the workshop in **Room T**, where a painstaking reconstruction is bringing three panels of Hans Memling's *Christ* *with Singing and Music-making Angels* back to glorious life, then head for the central galleries and – you guessed it – **Rubens**. The vast canvases on show were commissioned to hang in Antwerp churches, and their sheer size prevented the Spanish, Austrians and French from pilfering them, as they did so many other Flemish masterpieces. This is the artist at his most expressive and extravagant: masses of rippling, muscular bodies, thoughtful faces, tactile fabrics and dramatic contrasts in lighting; *Christ on the Cross* is especially bleak. The huge hall is flanked by galleries devoted to Rubens' most distinguished disciples, Jacob Jordaens and Anthony Van Dyck.

Downstairs, **Rooms 21-27** house a great survey of Belgian art from the late 19th and early 20th centuries. The star here is James Ensor, a half-English, Ostend-based artist who started out painting seascapes and sleepy bourgeois interiors, then mutated into something altogether more disturbing: a proto-expressionist, proto-surrealist, blending Beckmannesque critiques of social chit-chat with Boschian body horror. In *The Intrigue* (1890), masked middle-class grotesques cackle at an unknown joke (you really feel that it's on you); in *Adam and Eve Expelled from Paradise*, God is a bestial blur of electric energy, while Adam and Eve are cowed, shamed blobs of pink, forced into a sea of mud and rotting vegetation. Two self-portraits sum up Ensor: one shows a handsome, exquisitely whiskered artist with palette; the other, a jocular skeleton at the easel in the midst of his studio.

At the opposite extreme, there's a moving sequence of pictures by Rik Wouters, who died at 34. His bright, bold colours reveal a fauvist bent, but what marks him out is his ability to be tender without lapsing into tweeness. In a room devoted to nudes, his study of a long-haired woman has a rude energy and realism, and his portraits of his wife, Nel, are suffused with love and wonder; she's not beautiful, but she's made so by his vision. As a choking counterpoint, a self-portrait with eye patch from 1915 (he lost the sight in one eye as the result of a tumour that would kill him a year later), is drained of vitality, drenched in a dull, angry red, as if the artist cannot come to terms with the sadness of the world.

Other highlights include: powerful peasant scenes by the doughty Flemish expressionist Constant Permeke; arch-melancholic Léon Spilliaert's ghostly *Self-Portrait with Book* (Ibsen or Kafka, no doubt); René Magritte's sly sculptural update of David's *Madame Recamier*, in which the subject is replaced by a sitting-up coffin, bent in the middle; Paul Delvaux's dreamy surrealist landscapes, littered with wide-eyed nudes and leering skeletons; and colourful post-war abstracts by Jef Verheyen.

On leaving the museum, look out for the vast black bench, an incomplete circle designed by Ann Demeulemeester. Round the back, there's a block of glorious art nouveau houses, the 'Five Continents', constructed for a shipbuilder; a wooden prow juts out proudly beneath the glass-topped balcony. A little further south, at De Bouwmeesterstraat 7, is a splendid synagogue dating from 1893.

Lambermontplaats
Map 1, G1, p250

Unless you're obsessed with 19th-century town houses, this is a pleasant but uneventful square – except on the last Sunday of spring and summer months, when it hosts **Lambermontmartre** (May-Sep 1200-1700), an upbeat art fair with kiosks selling snacks, beer and Pernod. The art isn't amazing, but it's a lively, local affair.

Vlaamse Kaai and Waalse Kaai
Map 2, H1, p252

As the name suggests, this vast square was once home to two quays, the Flemish and the Walloon (named after Belgium's francophone southern region, Wallonia). Wedged between Leopold de Waelplaats and the river, it's now the epicentre of the Zuid, thanks to its appealing combination of powerhouse cultural institutions and pulsating bars and clubs. The monumental gate at the southern end of the Waalse Kaai was built in 1624, and moved from the city centre only in 1936.

Zuiderpershuis

*Waalse Kaai 14, **T** 03-248 7077, www.zuiderpershuis.be. Map 2, H1, p252*

The city's 'world cultural centre' is housed in a vast former power station, erected in 1883 in a fabulously rugged neo-medieval style. Behind its imposing twin towers, you'll find a multi-purpose modern arts venue, with regular concerts and theatre and dance performances by artists from across the globe. There are temporary photo exhibitions in the foyer (Wed-Sun), which also houses a cracking café.

Museum van Hedendaagse Kunst Antwerpen (Museum of Contemporary Art Antwerp)

*Leuvenstraat 32, **T** 03-238 5960, www.muhka.be. Tue-Sun 1000-1700. €5. Map 1, F1, p250*

Muhka, as it's universally known, is Antwerp's biggest showcase for contemporary art (from 1970 onwards). Housed in a squat art deco grain silo, it's a vast white-walled space with temporary shows on the ground floor and rotating displays of the permanent holdings upstairs. By its nature, it presents artists you probably haven't heard of, but recent acquisitions include works by Douglas Gordon, Mona Hatoum, Rebecca Horn and Luc Tuymans, which should give you a sense of what to expect. When gallery fatigue sets in, head for the café, where a cheery Keith Haring piece covers one wall.

White hot art
A converted grain silo provides a showcase for contemporary art at Muhka.

FotoMuseum
*Waalse Kaai 47, **T** 03-242 9300, www.fotomuseum.be. Tue-Sun 1000-1700. €6. Map 1, off F1, p250*

Yet another warehouse conversion (once a storage space for cheese), with a new wing designed by the architect Georges Baines, the Photography Museum is a pristine white space with terribly trendy toilets. It possesses one of Europe's most extensive image collections, although a bafflingly small fraction of those holdings is actually on show. To compensate, there's a charming display of early cameras, magic lanterns and projectors, the showpiece being the room-sized, many-seated Kaizerkamer, in which you can see old pictures of Antwerp zoo. Temporary shows explore the development of certain genres – reportage, advertising, fashion – or showcase emerging and established talents.

On the same site is the **Film Museum** (**T** 03-242 9357, www.muhka.be/film), with art house programmes, as well as the more experimental Muhka cinema.

Justitiepaleis
Bolivarplaats. Map 1, G1, p250

As you head south down Volkstraat, or wait for a tram on Leopold de Waelplaats, you can't fail to notice the assortment of white funnels on the horizon: these belong to the city's latest architectural icon, the new, eco-friendly law courts, designed by Richard Rogers. Long before completion, these "geometric hyperbolic paraboloid forms" had earned an array of comparisons – upturned ice-cream cones, futuristic oast houses, Ku Klux Klan hats – but most locals have settled on the 'Mohican'. The rest of the building is less radical, at least to the untrained eye, but the new concentration of lawyers should see a rush of restaurant openings in this hitherto dreary part of town.

Antwerpse Miniatuurstad
*Hangar 15, Cockerillkaai 50, **T** 03-237 0329, www.miniatuurstad.be. Daily 1000-1700. €6.50. Map 1, off F1, p250*

Opened in the 1980s by a skilled model-maker, this cheerily cheesy attraction gives you an overview of the city's history and includes models of most of the city's important buildings, including its only Le Corbusier house, owned by fashion designer Ann Demeulemeester. The visit ends with a bizarre son et lumière, to the music from *Chariots of Fire*, thunderclaps and a soundtrack of ships' horns, squawking seagulls and cathedral bells. The burghers of Brussels would be horrified to hear Antwerp described as "the greatest city of Belgium", where you can "spend your time in an educative or frivolous way".

't Eilandje

*The 'Little Island' is not an island at all, but its succession of bridges, quays and marinas makes it feel separate from the rest of the city. Antwerp's main commercial harbour during the 19th century, this northern district is undergoing a sea change, as investment floods in to convert the vast warehouses and shipping HQs on the **Willemdok** into penthouses, office blocks and restaurants. The Royal Ballet of Flanders and the Philharmonic Orchestra are both based in the area; Antwerp Sixer Dries van Noten has his headquarters here; and the long-awaited **Museum aan de Stroom**, due for completion in 2008, should set the seal on the area's regeneration.*

*The **Kattendijkdok**, on the Eilandje's northern fringes, still has the feel of a working port; keep going north and you'll start to see the vast docks and warehouses of the modern harbour, which sprawls for miles up the banks of the Scheldt. And, if you find the Eilandje's new look a little too neat, you'll get a better sense of gritty port life in the southern **Schipperskwartier**, where dockers and sailors lived, drank and fought; still run-down in stretches, it's now the epicentre of the city's red-light district.*

▸▸ *See Sleeping p131, Eating p153, Bars and clubs p168*

⊙ Sights

Bonapartedok and Willemdok
Map 1, D11, p251

The city's oldest extant docks were constructed on the orders of Napoleon. When Boney occupied Antwerp in 1794 (the place struck him as extremely ugly, by all accounts), he was welcomed as a saviour who would renew the long-stagnating city. His intention, however, was rather more sinister: he wanted the docks to be a "pistol pointed at the heart of England".

▶ Exploring the port

The best way to appreciate the sheer size of the port is to drive around it (there's a 70 km port route, with an exhaustively detailed brochure in English available at the tourist office for €1.50). It is a humbling experience, and no amount of statistics can convey how it feels to crawl through endless stretches of industrial activity, past monstrously large lorries, cranes with giant jaws, lake-sized docks, enormous containers and seemingly endless rows of refineries, a reminder that Antwerp's petrochemical plant is second only to Houston's. You really feel as though you shouldn't be here, an effect only amplified by heightened security in the wake of 9/11.

Even more dislocating are the occasional traces of the old polder villages that have been swallowed up by the ever-expanding port: every so often, you'll see a church tower nestling between warehouses. For a (slightly packaged) sense of how things were before, visit sleepy **Lillo**, an amazingly quiet little village, with a small but welcome public garden, a mini marina and a disproportionate number of restaurants. Further north, there's even a nature reserve, the **Reigersbos**, famous for its blue herons.

After Waterloo, the Dutch briefly assumed control of Antwerp. Fearing that it might rival Rotterdam, King Willem I did little to improve the port, and the Dutch kept the Scheldt closed after Belgium acquired independence in 1830. Only in 1863, when the restrictions on the river were lifted, could the city flourish – and flourish it did.

Today, these docks are the heart of the new Eilandje, with scrubbed cobbled pavements, newly planted trees, a sprinkling of benches, pretty wrought-iron lamps – and the inevitable loft apartments, cafés and restaurants. Take a seat and admire the old

▶ Port portrait

Vincent Van Gogh's correspondence with his brother, Theo, during his stay in Antwerp offers a vivid impression of the harbour in its heyday: "This morning I made a long walk in the pouring rain, a journey which had as its goal to get my stuff from the customs office; the different entrepôts and hangars at the quays are very beautiful. It is an impenetrable chaos… the figures are always moving, one sees the most peculiar entourages, everything jagged, and every time, automatically, there originate interesting contradictions. A white horse in the mud, in a corner where heaps of goods are covered under canvas – against old walls, black from the smoke, in the depot.

"One will look through the window of a very elegant English pub… There will be Flemish sailors with exaggeratedly healthy faces and broad shoulders, powerful and full and Antwerp through and through, eating mussels or drinking… There comes a very small figure in black with hands against her body inaudibly sneaking past the grey walls… It's a Chinese girl, mysteriously silent like a mouse – small, bedbug-like in character. What a contrast with the group of Flemish mussel-eaters!"

wooden hangars and the red and yellow brick warehouses across the water: the 19th-century **Sint-Felix Warehouse** (Godefriduskaai 30), a listed building, has been a storehouse for everything from coffee, honey and Parmesan to wine and tobacco.

Brouwershuis

*Adriaan Brouwerstraat 20, **T** 03-236 6511, museum.antwerpen.be/ brouwershuis. By appointment only, €2. Map 1, A3, p250*

Harbour master
For over 1000 years, the river Scheldt has been the key to the city's prosperity.

Built in the 16th century, the Brewers' House was not actually a brewery (nor was it the home of the carousing artist who gave the street its name). It was, in fact, a horse-powered watermill, designed by the engineer and property speculator Gilbert Van Schoonbeke, and acquired its name from the local breweries that it supplied. You can still see the ancient pipes and machinery, the stables and the meeting rooms used by the Brewers' Guild from 1582.

Belgisch Loodswezen
Tavernierkaai 3. Map 1, A3, p250

Built in 1896, the neo-Gothic headquarters of the river pilots were intended to remind those arriving by boat of Antwerp's new-found wealth and importance. Plans are afoot to convert it into a luxury riverside hotel. There's a statue of Brabo (see page 38) on the gable and, outside, a monument to seamen who lost their lives in the two world wars, dubbed 'Wrong Way Jeff' because his boots would normally have been covered by trousers (the artist wanted to show off the skilfully sculpted footwear).

Rijnkaai
Map 1, B10, p251

Now windswept and slightly desolate, with just a few rusting cranes on the quayside, the Rhine Quay was once a theatre of dreams and disappointment. This was the departure point for the Red Star Line, which carried millions of people, many of them Jews fleeing persecution in Eastern Europe, to the USA and Canada between 1873 and 1935. Embarkation was a rowdy, emotional affair, with Ellis Island the next stop for many travellers. Pickpockets and prostitutes mingled with the crowds, and many would-be emigrants placed their savings in the hands of ticket touts, only to see their hopes turn to dust.

The Red Star Line's return leg was usually less dramatic, but that was not the case in March 1933, when Albert Einstein and his wife, Elsa, stepped off a ship on the Rijnkaai. The physicist was en route to his native Germany after a Stateside lecture tour, but news of a crackdown on Jews prompted him to tell journalists that it was now impossible for him to return. His possessions had already been confiscated. He eventually emigrated, via England, to the USA.

Under the aegis of the Museum aan de Stroom project (see p90), the Red Star Line warehouse is to become a memorial for the refugees, with an exhibition of paintings by port artist Eugeen Van Mieghem (1875-1930), who captured the harsh reality of life on the waterfront, as lived by the porters, dockers and down-and-outs.

● *As the river bends, look back for a fine view of the city skyline – for many passengers, this would have been a last glimpse of Europe.*

Kattendijkdok
Map 1, B11, p251

As you head north, the bend of the Scheldt marks the end of Antwerp city and the beginning of the port proper. The two begin to merge around the Kattendijkdok, a long, thin rectangular dock established in 1858. This is a paradise for aficionados of industrial architecture, and the street names have a suitably global feel: on Montevideostraat, you'll see the white-stone ornamentation of the Montevideo Warehouses. The sloping roofs, which faced north to block out sunlight, provided cool storage even in the hottest weather. Mexicostraat leads to the Mexicobrug, a steel 1930s bridge with a wonderful lifting mechanism that marks the boundary with the commercial docks. On **Siberiastraat**, in splendid isolation, stands the Pomphuis, which pumped water to the dry dock where Red Star Line ships were repaired and maintained: it's been converted into a spectacular restaurant (see Eating, p153).

Extra City
*Mexicostraat-Kattendijkdok, Kaai 44, **T** 0484-421070, www.extra city.org. Wed-Sun 1100-1800, Sun 1100-2300. €3. Map 1, A11, p251*

The decrepit-looking brick grain silo at the northern tip of the Kattendijkdok is now home to one of the city's most exciting exhibition spaces. The rugged grey walls give a gritty, industrial feel, and make a great change from sterile white; the temporary exhibitions are unrelentingly avant-garde; and the slightly unnerving sensation that the building might collapse at any moment only adds to the transgressive feel. As if that weren't enough, Extra City houses the fabulous **Fake Bar** (see p168) and Antwerp's most unusual accommodation, **Hotelit** (see p131).

Port Police Station
Bordeauxstraat. Map 1, C11, p251

Back in the southern section of 't Eilandje, you'll find the port's first police HQ. It was known as the 'Blood Shack', an indication of how rough alcohol-fuelled life on the waterfront could be. As port history expert Pit de Jonge explains: "Employers believed that hard labour had to be supported by drinking, and 'jenever' (Dutch gin) was praised for its medicinal properties." Rather cynically, the bars were often owned by the employers…

The first recruitment centre for dock workers and ship repair labourers stood on the corner of Rigastraat and Napelsstraat. This was the scene of violent confrontations during the 1907 dockers' strike, when British port labourers were greeted with the slogan: "English rats, roll your mats!" Around the corner, the neo-Gothic **Workers' Shelter** (Londenstraat 52) was built in 1908 to give labourers somewhere to wash, sup and keep out of trouble. Once an alcohol-free zone, it now houses, somewhat ironically, a trendy restaurant (La Riva, see p153).

Museum aan de Stroom
Hanzestedenplaats, www.museumaandestroom.antwerpen.be.
Expected to open Spring 2008. Map 1, D11, p251

A decade in the making, the 'museum on the river' is a typically ambitious Antwerp project. Located in a boldly contemporary, Jenga-style complex on the site of the Hansa League's 16th-century headquarters, it will unite the collections of the Vleeshuis, the Steen and the Folklore museum to tell the story of Antwerp, its port and its people over the past millennium. Expect all the latest interactive bells and whistles – and a spanking new café.

Zurenborg

Showy, extravagant, theatrical, deluded? No thesaurus could do justice to the flamboyance of Cogels-Osylei, the weird, wide avenue at the Zurenborg's heart. A riot of historical pastiche and progressive art nouveau, it's perhaps the most remarkable, ridiculous architectural ensemble in Europe, and could only be a product of the late 19th century. Its incongruity is heightened by its proximity to unlovely

*Berchem station, the city's international rail hub. The surrounding area bears the telltale marks of gentrification, but remains more ragged and bohemian than the ultra-smooth Zuid. The once waterlogged terrain of the Zurenborg ('Acid Town' was named for the pH properties of its soil) was partly reclaimed by poplar planting in the 16th century. Sharing borders with the Jewish district and, to the northwest, Borgerhout, the area is ethnically and socially diverse: on the main square, the café-lined **Dageraadplaats**, you'll see Jewish families in the playground and Arab youths playing basketball.*

▸▸ See Sleeping p132, Eating p154, Bars and clubs p171

◉ Sights

★ Cogels-Osylei
Map 1, H10, p251

You'd be forgiven for thinking this was a film set someone forgot to dismantle – but no, these are real buildings, commissioned without irony by some of fin-de-siècle Antwerp's wealthiest citizens. There's an unwritten rule in Belgium that no two buildings on a street can look the same, and this broad boulevard takes that principle to hilarious extremes. Imitation Gothic turrets, fake Tudor timbering, French châteaux, onion domes, a Venetian palazzo, Greek temples – they're all here, making the art nouveau buildings look almost austere. You can get the idea without a guidebook, but architecture fans should pick up the excellent 'Zurenborg Walk' brochure, available at the tourist office. It's full of useful detail, including a list of the houses with floral, animal, astrological or mythical names.

Heading from Tramplein towards Berchem station, you could do the following **circular walk**. Start on **Cogels-Osylei**, taking in the Roman palace with a golden statue of Charlemagne (6-12); the Italianate neo-Renaissance palazzo, with a loggia and a statue

> ### Discreet charm of the bourgeoisie?

Perhaps the most entertaining thing about Cogels-Osylei is that the original residents took great pride in flaunting their wealth and (often egregious) taste. The land was bought by an influential Catholic politician, Baron Osy de Zichen, in 1837; his daughter married John Cogels, who set up a company called the Corporation for the Construction of Middle-class Residences to develop the domain and build fancy villas for the bourgeoisie. (Until 1929, only professional gardeners were allowed to tend the front gardens!) However, after the Second World War, owners increasingly found these grandiose properties too expensive and difficult to maintain, and in the late 1960s, many contemplated selling up as the price of land soared thanks to the new Berchem railway terminus. There were plans to demolish the luxury piles, replacing them with modern residences. Then the protests began, artists and intellectuals moved in, and, thankfully, the ensemble was saved.

of Apollo (19-23); and the neo-Flemish Renaissance Stars, Sun and Moon (25-29). Take a detour to **General Capiaumontstraat**, in search of the pseudo-temple with door handles shaped like Olympic torches (2-4). Then, back on Cogels, check out the swirling art nouveau patterns of De Zonnebloem (Sunflower, 50); the ironwork and mosaics of the Tulip (52); a beehive bas-relief (70-72); the Venetian palazzo, with statues of Poseidon and Amphitrite (67-69); and the remarkable wrought-iron balcony at Quinten Matsijs (80).

Turn sharp right into **Waterloostraat**, via Guldenvliesstraat, to admire Den Tijd (The Time, 59), with mosaics devoted to different times of day; the mosaic of seagulls at Les Mouettes (39); and De Slag van Waterloo (Battle of Waterloo, 11), with portraits of Wellington and Napoleon. You then come to **Transvaalstraat**, named in memory of the Boer War, where you can admire the sgraffiti-rich façade of De Twaalf Apostelen (12 Apostles, 13-17); the pediments and obelisks of the Grieks Tempel (Greek Temple, 23-33); Greco-Roman statuary (23-37); the gorgeous lemon and turquoise flower motifs of the Lotus (52); and the sculpted devils of De Twaalf Duivels (12 Devils, 59-61).

The last word goes to Frans Brenders, writing in *Zurenborg Belle Epoque* (see p237). Brenders sees this glorious jumble of architecture – what he pithily calls the "delirium tremens style" – as "typical of Antwerp people, who stubbornly ignore their descent into provincialism, preferring instead to cultivate their legendary grandiosity".

Draakplaats
Map 1, G9, p251

On the other side of Tramplein, things calm down a little, though the original headquarters of the Antwerp Tramway Company (1904) show how elaborate public-transport buildings used to be. Look out for the two Moorish-style water towers next to the railway line, and for the high double doors that open to reveal a tram depot. Turn left into **Grote Hondstraat**, into a district where streets and villas are named after the firmament: Grote Beerstraat (Great Bear), Walvisstraat (Whale), Schorpioenstraat (Scorpio). Wind up at **Dageraadplaats** (Sunrise Square), a charmingly scruffy social hub with a happy mix of old-fashioned and new cafés and restaurants.

Borgerhout

This once prosperous suburb is now somewhat dusty and disheavelled, starved of green spaces despite having the highest concentration of children in the city. About 20% of the population is of northwest African origin – the Belgian and Moroccan governments agreed a labour-for-materials deal in the late 1950s – and the decline of industry has left many out of work. The resulting tensions have led the less enlightened to call the area 'Borgerocco', a racist term that second-generation Moroccans have defiantly adopted as their own. The level of support for the extreme right is alarmingly high, but middle-class, left-leaning, community-oriented Borgerhoutenaren are also making their presence felt. There are growing signs of urban regeneration, thanks to the lefties and to the growing number of artists and intellectuals, drawn by cheap rents, decent architecture and a new buzz in the air. In June, Borgerhout organizes an **Open House** *festival, in which residents open their homes and work spaces to the public. This neighbourhood is also home to the state-run* **Ecohuis** *and to some genuinely boho bars. All it lacks is a museum of immigration.*

▸▸ *See Sleeping p132, Eating p155, Bars and clubs p172*

◉ Sights

Stadhuis
Moorkensplein 1. Tram 10, 24. Map, 1, E10, p251

Amid some rather dreary post-war architecture, it's a delightful surprise to happen on the palatial neo-Renaissance town hall, built in the late 19th century to reflect Borgerhout's dynamism and importance. The interior, with vaulted roofing, is equally impressive. Nearby **Oedenkovenstraat** was one of the wealthier streets. Ahead, towards the Centraal station, you can see the yellow-brick houses built in the 1950s and 1960s

▶ Day trips from Antwerp

★ Middelheim Sculpture Park, Middelheimlaan 61, T 03-827 1534. *Oct-Mar 1000-1700, Apr-Sep 1000-1900, May and Aug 1000-2000. Jun-Jul 1000-2100. Closed Mon. Free; audioguide €3. From Centraal station or Roosenvelt plaats, take bus 501 or 502 (stop Lindendreef-Middelheimlaan, the stop before Middelheim Hospital).* In a city starved of green spaces, this pretty, peaceful park would be worth a visit on its own – so the addition of dozens of sculptures by some of modern art's biggest names seems almost indecently generous. As you stroll beneath copper beeches and monkey puzzle trees, you'll see figurative and abstract works by Rodin, Henry Moore, Barbara Hepworth, Alexander Calder and Jean Arp, among many others. Some take pride of place on the immaculate lawns, others are hidden, delightfully, amid the trees. Bring a picnic if you want to make a day of it.

Arboretum Kalmthout, Heuvel 2, Kalmthout, T 03-666 6741, www.arboretum kalmthout.be. *Mid Jan-mid Feb and mid Mar-mid Nov, daily 1000-1700. €4, children €1.50. Bus 12 or train from Antwerpen-Centraal to Roosendaal, alight at Kalmthout station.* This is Antwerp's answer to Kew Gardens, an English-style park where visitors are encouraged to walk on the grass and take a close look at the trees, shrubs and spectacular colours. Botany buffs should look out for an endangered species of Chinese conifer, which flames dramatically in autumn, one of the world's last snowdrop trees and the largest collection of witchhazel on the continent, which attracts tourists from as far as Japan in winter, when it flowers. Cyclists should get off the train at Kapellen, an affluent northern suburb, then cycle next to the railway line, through the woods to Kalmthout itself.

Day trips (continued)

Fort Breendonk Brandstraat 57, Willebroek, **T** 03-860 7525, www.breendonk.be. *Daily 0930-1730. €6. Free parking. Train to Mechelen, then a train towards Sint-Niklaas; get off at Willebroek.* Used as a prison by the Gestapo, this forbidding fortress has been turned into a museum and memorial to the victims of Nazi rule in Belgium. It's a grim reminder of mankind's limitless capacity for cruelty, with few tales of resilience to cushion the experience as you visit the cells, the cramped bedrooms, the latrines and the torture room, fitted with drains for urine and blood. The video displays and unflinching audio commentary, with testimonies from former inmates, leave nothing to the imagination.

The fort itself is clammy and claustrophobic, so it's something of a relief when you emerge – until you see the execution place, and the moat where a teenage boy once cried for his mother while guards hurled him into freezing water until he died.

Kanaal Stokerijstraat 15-19, Wijnegem, **T** 03-355 3300, www.axel-vervoordt.com. *Thu-Fri 1400-1800, Sat 1100-1800. Bus 411 from Kongingin Astridplein to Wijnegem. A taxi would cost €20-25.* Axel Vervoordt, art dealer extraordinaire, displays his impeccably chosen art and antiques in this former industrial complex beyond the city. It's a labyrinth of nooks, echoing halls and corridors, with furniture, contemporary art, lamps and mirrors on show. The lighting is dramatic, too, suddenly revealing a 13th-century Chinese statue of a priest or an abstract painting by the Belgian artist Jef Verheyen. The highlight is Anish Kapoor's *At the End of the World* (revealed only on request): a dark, round space with a wine-red dome and extraordinary acoustics.

Time your visit to coincide with an open day at Vervoordt's home, Kasteel van 's Graven-wezel, Sint-Jobsteenweg 64, 's Gravenwezel, **T** 03-658 1470.

following extensive bombing during the Second World War. **Kroonstraat 49** was built by a butcher who was granted the right to supply meat to Belgium's royal family after he lent his umbrella to the king during a public ceremony. The statue on top depicts the medieval butcher, Jan Breydel. Cross busy, noisy Turnhoutsebaan to **Kerkstraat**, dominated by a neo-Romanesque church and lined with arty bars and restaurants where you'll see off-duty members of Jan Fabre's theatre company; the avant garde guru has a studio up the road.

De Roma

*Turnhoutsebaan 286, **T** 03-235 0490, www.deroma.be. Tram 10, 24. Map 1, E11, p251*

This art deco cinema with a beautiful blue-glass entrance roof, patterned with circles, was built in 1928 by a Naples-born entrepreneur, Mr Romeo, an illiterate mason who worked his way up with dogged determination. The name is made up of the first two letters of his name and that of his Hungarian-born wife, Malev. Long abandoned, it has been lovingly restored by local volunteers and is now a characterful cultural space with excellent acoustics and a real buzz about it. As well as screening films, it hosts jazz, pop and classical concerts, dance and theatre, and is an 'in' destination even for people who would otherwise never go near Borgerhout.

Ecohuis

*Turnhoutsebaan 139, **T** 03-217 0811, www.eha.be. Tue-Sun 1000-1630. €2, Fri free. Tram 10, 24. Map 1, D10, p251*

The modern wood façade of the Ecological House, a homage to sustainable living, stands out a mile on this shabby thoroughfare. Delightfully, as you approach the building, the traffic noise disappears, as if by magic, and is replaced by the gentle sound of running water – a fountain in front forms a sound screen between the house and the main road.

Created by the City of Antwerp with EU backing, the Ecohuis displays green-themed exhibitions and permanent displays about the environment. A pebbled path through the pretty garden leads to a sustainable show house (rainwater is used for the toilets; solar panels provide the power) in which you can stay overnight (see p132). Or relax on the café terrace (see p155), watching – but not hearing – the world go by.

Luchtschipbouw

Karel Geertsstraat 2b, **T** *03-271 0667, www.panamarenko.be. Wed-Sat 1400-1800. Map 1, D12, p251*

There is no clearer sign of regeneration – or, as Asterix might say, no better evidence that the Belgians are crazy – than this former electricity building, now a vast white exhibition space for the eccentric work of Panamarenko. The self-styled "artist, engineer, poet, physicist, inventor and visionary" has found international fame thanks to his improbable flying machines – Heath Robinson fans will be in seventh heaven – with fantastic faux-sci-fi names (Bing of the Ferro Lusto?). For one exhibition, a bird dealer with hundreds of cages provided the background music.

● *Nearby, the* **Krugerpark** *was developed in the 1980s to encourage families to return to a greener Borgerhout.*

Historic centre

You don't have to look hard to find the glories of medieval Ghent: at the city's heart is a string of showpiece squares and spires, stretching from the austere Sint-Niklaaskerk, via the dragon-topped belfry, to Sint-Baafskathedraal, home of Van Eyck's miraculous Lamb of God. Though there's plenty of bustle on the Korenmarkt, the main transport hub, it's easy to find quiet side streets lined with gabled houses, or peaceful waterfront stretches. Ghent's trading power is evoked by the Graslei, a stunning ensemble of riverside guild houses spanning several centuries and styles; tranquil Jan Breydelstraat is home to the Design Museum, a showcase for interiors and artefacts past and present; round the corner looms the Gravensteen castle, much restored, but still authentically forbidding.

Sint-Baafskathedraal
Sint-Baafsplein, **T** 09-269 2045. *Apr-Oct 0830-1800; Nov-Mar 0830-1700; free. Mystic Lamb Apr-Oct 0930-1645; Nov-Mar 1030-1545; €2.50. Map 3, H6, p255*

A rugged, slightly hulking structure, the exterior of St Bavo's Cathedral lacks the poise and polish of its counterpart in Antwerp, but inside it's a different story. A beautiful blend of French and Flamboyant Gothic (the first in blue stone, the second in white), it's crammed with priceless treasures: a remarkable wooden pulpit, inspired by the Tree of Knowledge and topped off with a golden serpent; the coats of arms of the Knights of the Golden Fleece, convened by Philip II in 1559; a baroque 17th-century organ, the largest in the Benelux; a theatrical Rubens, the *The Conversion of St Bavo*, in which the former dissolute gives up his worldly possessions and prepares to lead a new life as a monk.

   Put all those treasures on hold, though, because you're here for one thing above all others: *The Adoration of the Mystic Lamb*, Ghent's most prized possession and one of western civilization's

The Adoration of the Mystic Lamb

If every picture is worth 1000 words, you'd need a fat book to do justice to the *Mystic Lamb*'s 20 panels, 250 figures and more than 40 types of flower – indeed, as the *Penguin Dictionary of Art & Artists* puts it, "more ink has been spilt [on it] than on any other subject in the history of art". There's much controversy over whether this was the work of Van Eyck, or a collaboration, possibly posthumous, with his brother Hubert, who may or may not have existed.

Perhaps most remarkable, however, is that the work is still in Ghent, and more or less intact. Philip II wanted to move it to Spain; Joseph II, fresh from telling Mozart that his work contained "too many notes", decided that the Adam and Eve panels contained too much nudity, and had copies made in which the couple are clothed (you'll see these on your way out). Napoleon nicked it during the occupation of Ghent by revolutionary forces;

remarkably, the city got it back, but the outer wings were promptly sold to a Berlin museum, only to be returned a century later as reparation for damage caused in World War One.

So, the panels were once again reunited – but not for long. In 1934, a thief stole the Just Judges panel, recently back from Berlin, with a portrait of St John the Baptist on its back; the latter was deposited in a left-luggage locker, together with a ransom demand. The Just Judges panel has never been recovered – the version in the cathedral is a copy from 1941 – although it does turn up in Albert Camus' *The Fall*, in the narrator's wardrobe. The Nazis removed the *Lamb* on Hitler's orders, and it was found after the war in an Austrian salt mine. Since then, it's stayed in its rightful place… or almost: in 1986, it was moved to the baptistry from the cathedral's 13th-century chapel. We're lucky to have it at all.

finest achievements. A vast, impossibly luminous altarpiece completed by Jan van Eyck in 1432, it took realism to as-yet undreamt-of levels: almost a century later, its astounding use of the then newly discovered oil paints left the great Albrecht Dürer scratching his head in wonder, and the glowing colours still look fresh, even newly applied, today. You could spend hours lost in admiration of Mary's face, or the cut of Christ's cloak.

Before you leave, pop down to the intimate, vaulted Romanesque crypt, its walls embellished with 15th- and 16th-century frescoes. Until spring 2007, you'll see a selection of works from the city's Fine Arts Museum (see p113) – in particular Hieronymus Bosch's *Bearing of the Cross*, a bleak close-up of the Calvary cortège in which the dignity and pathos of Christ's face is in almost unbearable contrast to the gallery of leering, venal grotesques who crowd in on him.

Het Belfort

Botermarkt. *Mar-Nov, daily 1000-1230 and 1400-1730; Easter and May-Sep, daily 1410, 1520 and 1620, 45-minute guided tour. €5. Map 3, G5, p255*

The belfry, on which construction began in 1314, is the soaring symbol of Ghent's civic autonomy and is topped by a glittering gilded dragon, a suitably fierce defender of the city's liberties. The spire was made over for the 1913 World Fair. Climb the dingy steps of the tower (or take the glass lift) for a superb view of the city, passing huge ancient bells as you ascend: the Roeland bell weighs a whopping 6000 kg. If you're lucky, the 54-bell carillon might explode into action as you negotiate your way onto the parapet.

Back on terra firma, the heavily renovated 15th-century **Lakenhalle** (Cloth Hall), adjacent to the tower, is now home to the tourist office; and, round the back, you'll find a bizarre carving of an elderly man sucking eagerly at the breasts of a young woman. Before you get any ideas, this is Cimon, condemned to death by starvation, and fed breast milk by his daughter to keep him going.

Bats in the belfry?

Street entertainers keep visitors amused on Sint-Baafsplein during the Gentse Feesten, see p191.

★ **Romantic spots in Ghent**

Best

- **Lievekaai**, p107.
- **Appelbrug** (but only if there's no one else there), p108.
- **Sint-Pietersabdij** herb garden, p111.
- **Citadelpark** bandstand, p112.
- **Jan Breydel** restaurant, p156.

Sint-Niklaaskerk

Cataloniëstraat, **T** 09-225 3700. *Mon 1400-1700, Tue-Sun 1000-1700. Map 3, G3, p255*

This sober structure with a high, luminous, giddying interior is Flanders' finest example of Scheldt Gothic, an earlier and noticeably more austere style than the Flamboyant. Thanks to its proximity to the Korenmarkt and historic port, St Nicholas' became the place of worship for the city's wealthiest merchants and guilds. Its whitewashed interior, though still under renovation, is calm, harmonious and refreshingly cool in the summer heat.

Sint-Michielsbrug

Map 3, G2, p255

The three towers of Ghent – Sint-Bavo, the Belfry and Sint-Nicholas – are at their finest when viewed from the Gothic St Michael's Bridge. Well, Gothic-ish: it was built in the early 20th century to provide visitors with an unforgettable view of the newly spruced-up old town. To your left are the **guild houses** of **Graslei** and **Korenlei**; to your right is the neglected-looking **Sint-Michielskerk**, begun in 1440, but never finished; and, further down, **Het Pand**, a former Dominican friary that's now used as a conference centre by Ghent University. If you're wondering about the fourth tower, just behind the Graslei, it belongs to the former post office, built, inevitably, in 1913 for the World Fair.

Graslei and Korenlei
Map 3, F2 & F2, p254

These two quaysides, in use since the 11th century, constitute Ghent's first commercial port. From here boats could follow the River Leie, via Damme, to the North Sea; now the only traffic here is the steady stream of puttering tourist boats (see p27). The Graslei is the more elegant of the two, with a stunning parade of step-gabled guild houses: look out for the **Guild of the Free Boatmen** (No 14), in Flamboyant Gothic style; the sculpted scrolls of the **Coorenmetershuys** (Corn Measurers' House; Nos 12-13); the tiny Renaissance-style **Tollhouse** (No 11); and the Romanesque limestone **Staple House**, built around 1200 (No 10).

Many of the merchants' houses on the Korenlei have been demolished, but you can still see the rich, stuccoed façade of the **Guild of Unfree Boatmen**, topped with a golden boat (only those born in the city had the right to navigate the city's inner waterways; others were restricted, or 'unfree'", and had to use the free boatmen to transfer their cargoes into the city). The view from the **Grasbrug**, which links the quays at their northern end, is particularly beautiful at night, when lights are reflected in the still canals. In fine weather, the quays are buzzing at all hours, with packed café terraces and students hanging out over takeaway pizza and beer at the water's edge.

Groot Vleeshuis
Groentenmarkt, **T** 09-267 8607, www.grootvleeshuis.be. *Tue-Sun, 1000-1800. Map 3, D3, p254*

On the old vegetable market, the city's first commercial centre, the 15th-century Great Butchers' Hall, with decorative step gables

Reflected glory
The gabled guild houses along the Korenlei and Graslei are a reminder of Ghent's past as a prosperous medieval river port.

above its elegant high windows, is a fitting showcase for the finest regional produce. Cured hams hang from the huge wooden beams, and you can sample and buy Flemish cheeses, jams and aperitifs. Head east to admire the old houses on **Hoogpoort**, then walk back across Sint-Veerleplein, pausing to admire the deliciously over-the-top baroque façade of the **Vismarkt**: for too long neglected, the building is set to become a cultural centre.

Gravensteen

Sint-Veerleplein, **T** 09-225 9306. *Apr-Sept daily 0900-1800; Oct-Mar daily 0900-1700. €6. Map 3, C2, p254*

The Castle of the Counts looks exactly the way you'd expect a medieval stronghold to – sombre, imposing, forbiddingly fortified – so it's perhaps a surprise that it's been altered many times down the centuries. There's been a fortress on this site for more than 1000 years, but its heyday as the city's seat of power was relatively short-lived: by the 15th century, Ghent's rulers preferred to stay in the Prinsenhof (see p115).

The castle then housed a mint – and a prison, with punishments and executions carried out on nearby Sint-Veerleplein or in the castle courtyard. During the reigns of Charles V and Philip II, the city's rebellious streak and enthusiasm for Calvinism ensured that the executioners were always kept busy. As a chilling reminder of these dark days, there's a display of instruments of torture – shackles, racks, branding irons and thumbscrews – which exercise a peculiar fascination for children. There's little reference, however, to the castle's stint as a textile factory.

Outside, you get great views of the city from the ramparts, where people in period dress do their best to recreate the medieval era.

● *Northwest of the castle, cross the Lievebrug to reach the* **Lievekaai** *(Map 3, B1, p254), one of the most romantic waterside locations in the city.*

Museum voor Sierkunst (Design Museum)
Jan Breydelstraat 5, **T** 09-267 9999, www.design.museum.gent.be.
Tue-Sun 1000-1800. €2.50.   Map 3, E 2, p254

A splendid patrician town house on one of Ghent's most charming streets serves as the Design Museum. There's an atmospheric old section and a new wing, in which the modern architecture blends perfectly with the exhibits. There are rooms recreating various periods and styles – baroque, rococo, Regency, Empire – in which the chandeliers, tortoiseshell cabinets, marquetry and mirrors are a feast for the eyes.

On the next floor, with ship-like white rails and huge windows, there's a splendid collection of art nouveau and art deco furniture and fittings, including a dazzling bookcase with copper trimmings by Paul Hankar, Gallé vases from Nancy, curvaceous chairs by Victor Horta and a complete art nouveau interior by Henry van de Velde. The top floor in the modern wing, where you can rest on seating by the British designer Jasper Morrison, is devoted to fanciful contemporary furniture, including a gaudy Milanese dressing table and stained-glass windows by a local designer, Herman Blondeel. One of the oddest items is an armchair made out of fabric bananas.

The museum also stages temporary exhibitions, with a range spanning Finnish glassware, 17th-century cabinets and Tupperware, while the shop sells suitably pricey designer items, including bags and silverware. More bizarrely, there's a gigantic sculpture of a toilet roll outside the building. It is indeed a toilet, and it's open to the public – given the shortage of public conveniences in the city centre, it's the ultimate in form and function.

● *The pretty riverside **Appelbrug**, at the Korenlei end of Jan Breydelstraat, is a perfect spot for a picnic.*

Vrijdagmarkt
Map 3, D5, p254

Once the centre of the city's political and social life, the site of executions and receptions, feuds and festivities, this vast open square is now lined with restaurants, shops and cafés. The most notable building is **Ons Huis** (1900), a stout structure in eclectic style that once housed the headquarters of the city's powerful Socialist Union. A statue of the 'Sage of Ghent', Jacob van Artevelde, who protected the textile trade by striving to maintain the city's neutrality during the Hundred Years' War, stands in the centre. The Gothic tower at No 37 belongs to the former **guild house of the Tanners**. Just off the square, on Groot Kanonplein, stands a cannon called **Dulle Griet** (Mad Meg), brought to Ghent in the 1570s to aid in the defence of the city against the Spanish, but apparently never fired successfully. Don't miss the **Hof van Ryhove**, at Onderstraat 22 (**T** 09-266 5326), a charming Renaissance town house with a pond and garden.

South of the historic centre

Ghent's character changes substantially as you walk down from the city centre: baroque and neoclassical buildings on calm, ordered streets replace the medieval muddle of the city's historic heart. The French influence is clear on the elegant Kouter, home of the opera house and a fine flower market on Sundays; cross the canal and you'll see the eclectic Vooruit building, formerly a flagship for Flemish socialism, now a cultural powerhouse. Towards the city's fringes, you'll find belle époque architecture and more baroque, this time in the restored Sint-Pietersabdij; continue south to the leafy Citadelpark for the bang up-to-date collection at SMAK, a heavyweight museum of contemporary art.

Kouter
Map 3, J4, p254

This broad square, lined with banks and elegant mansions, is a favourite place for a weekend stroll, especially on Sunday mornings, when it is filled with the colour and fragrance of the weekly flower market, and Gentenaars gather at the open-air stalls of De Blauwe Kiosk to wash down oysters with champagne. Wander through the fuchsias, begonias, vines and olive trees to the wrought-iron bandstand, where a brass ensemble bangs out standards such as *Fly Me to the Moon*.

It takes some imagination to picture the Kouter in medieval times, when archers of the Guild of St Sebastian held competitions to entertain visiting dignitaries. One of the finest houses is the rococo **Hotel Falligan** (No 172). West of the square stands the **opera house**; its sumptuous neoclassical interior is well worth a peek. South lies the **Ketelvest**, named after the adjacent canal, dug in the 11th and 12th centuries. Across the water, stroll along **Brabantdam** (there's a delightful courtyard at No 72) and the **Kuiperskaai**, another street that's on the rise, with trendy restaurants aplenty.

Vooruit
Sint-Pietersnieuwstraat 23. *See also p176.* *Map 3, off L6, p255*

This impressive structure, a blend of art nouveau and eclectic styles, was built by the architect of Ons Huis (see p109) as a meeting place for the Socialists just before the First World War. The name means 'Forward!', a typically optimistic slogan for this most progressive of cities. The Vooruit is now a top-class venue for dance, theatre and pop and classical concerts, as well as excellent weekend parties. Further south, look out for the red-tiled façade of the Vooruit's now-defunct newspaper office; the paper became *De Morgen*, Flanders' answer to *The Guardian*.

Sint-Pietersabdij

Sint-Pietersplein 9, **T** 09-243 9730, www.gent.be/spa. *Apr-Nov 1000-1800, last entry 1630. Free; video guide €7. Map 3, off L6 (off map), p255*

Although there's been an abbey on the site since at least the ninth century, the destructive urges of first the Vikings, then the Calvinist iconoclasts, explain why the domed church at the heart of this appealing complex is baroque in appearance. Now fully restored, the abbey is well worth a visit: there's even a working vineyard, something of a rarity in Flanders.

You can wander through the abbey, garden and ruins for free, but to get a more pungent sense of the place, pick up the interactive video guide, in which a virtual monk guides you round the buildings and through a gripping tale of love and murder. Your narrator is an amiable but melancholy Scottish-born Benedictine who extols the virtues of fine wines and good whisky while taking you to the chapel (where, if you're lucky, an organist will be rehearsing), the refectory, the attic and the herb garden.

Next door, the **Kunsthal Sint-Pietersabdij** hosts temporary art exhibitions. For a sharp change of pace, nearby **Overpoortstraat** lies at the heart of the student district.

De Wereld van Kina

Sint-Pietersplein 14, **T** 09-244 7373, www.dewereldvankina.be. *Mon-Fri 0900-1700, Sun 1400-1730. €2.50. Map 3, off L6 (off map), p255*

Located in a wing of the abbey, Ghent's natural history museum is aimed firmly at youngsters. It delves into geology, the evolution of life on earth, human biology and invertebrates – and, slightly off the subject, contains a scale model of the city in Charles V's day. A mini son et lumière show, also in English, recalls the rule of the Ghent-born emperor, who famously humiliated the local citizens by making them parade with nooses around their necks following a revolt against his taxation policy.

Citadelpark
Map 3, off L6 (off map), p255

As the name suggests, the city's largest green space was once the site of a fortress, erected by the Duke of Wellington in the wake of the Napoleonic wars. Little remains of the citadel now, though you'll see the odd trace amid the grottoes and rockeries; otherwise, this is a delightfully tranquil park, dotted with cascades, ponds, exotic trees and rose gardens. Don't miss the sumptuous white and green bandstand, decorated with pink angels and, bizarrely, encircled by roosters. On the surrounding streets, notably Charles de Kerchovelaan and Kunstlaan, you'll find handsome belle époque town houses with swirling coloured patterns on their façades.

Stedelijk Museum voor Actuele Kunst (SMAK)
Citadelpark, T 09-221 1703, www.smak.be. Tue-Sun 1000-1800. €5. Tram 1 to Kortrijksesteenweg. Map 3, off L6 (off map), p255

Founded by one of Europe's heavyweight curators, Jan Hoet, Ghent's contemporary art museum – or 'art of the moment,' as the name suggests – packs a real punch. Though it took Hoet 20 years to find a permanent home for the museum, in a former casino, his bold vision and eye for talent meant that the collection of post-war art he had amassed would rank as one of Europe's finest. To give just a flavour, it includes works by Carl Andre, Francis Bacon, Joseph Beuys, Christo, Dan Flavin, Lucio Fontana, Gilbert

! Jan Hoet, who once said that "if you don't understand boxing, you don't understand art", celebrated the inauguration of SMAK by sparring with the American artist Dennis A Bellone.

and George, David Hockney, Donald Judd, Anselm Kiefer, Sol LeWitt, Bruce Nauman, Gerhard Richter and Andy Warhol.

Not all the collection is on show, as the museum also makes generous space for temporary shows by the likes of Louise Bourgeois and Ilya Kabakov, rotating displays devoted to emerging artists and the Belgian biggies: look out for Marcel Broodthaers' mussel pots, Jan Fabre's iridescent beetle urinal, Luc Tuymans' Holocaust-inspired paintings and Wim Delvoye's Delftware-style gas canisters. The cool, high-ceilinged café provides welcome relief when all the postmodern playfulness becomes too wearing.

Museum voor Schone Kunsten (Museum of Fine Arts)
Charles de Kerchovelaan 187a, **T** 09-240 0700, www.msk.be.
Tue-Sun 1000-1800, Tram 1-10, stopping at
Kortrijksepoortstraat. Map 3, off L6 (off map), p255

Opposite SMAK is the Fine Arts Museum, a typically overblown neoclassical structure with monumental steps and columns. Though more conventional than its neighbour, it has several splendid works, most notably Bosch's *Bearing of the Cross* (see p102) and *St Jerome at Prayer*. Rubens and his protégés are also present, and there's a useful survey of Belgian artistic movements, including the Symbolists and the Sint-Martens-Latem schools (see p119), as well as a typically disturbing Ensor, *Skeleton looking at Chinoiserie*.

The museum is currently under renovation, and will reopen in spring 2007. Until then, you'll find highlights from the collection at other museums and monuments across the city, including the cathedral, MIAT and SMAK.

!
• Among the artist Jan Fabre's more unusual achievements was wrapping the pillars of the university with the local cured ham.

Sint-Pietersstation
Map 3, off L3 (off map), p255

Part Moorish, part Italianate, with loggias, pinkish brickwork, grey and green striped pillars and pictures of the city spires on the walls, Ghent's bizarre main station is something of an acquired taste. As observant readers will have guessed, it was built for the World Fair of 1913. It's a longish drag to the centre, so pick up tram No 1 – but spare a little time for the surrounding streets, which are dotted with showy art nouveau houses. There are splendid examples of sgraffiti, wrought-iron balconies and floral ceramic tiling on **Prinses Clementinalaan**, **Koningin Astridlaan** and **Oostendestraat**.

Bijloke Museum
Godshuizenlaan 2, **T** 09-225 1106. *Thu 1000-1300 and 1400-1800, Sun 1400-1800. €2.50.*

Housed in a Cistercian convent on the city's fringes, this sleepy historical museum takes you through Ghent's past up to the French Revolution, and is best appreciated when you already have a decent knowledge of the city and its leading lights. Most of the captions are in Dutch, with some in French. The collection includes furniture, porcelain and paintings, and there's a pleasant courtyard filled with ivy and apple trees.

Look out for a dramatic 19th-century watercolour showing Ghent's cathedral in flames, an 18th-century ink drawing of fireworks on the Vrijdagmarkt and a portrait of the pioneering psychologist Dr Jozef Guislain (see p118), looking suitably benign and reflective. The staircase is lined with wooden coats of arms, including that of the Free Boatmen, decorated with flags, ships and rigging. The dimly lit chapel, with black and terracotta flagstones, warm russet-coloured walls and a wooden roof, is a real treat, worth the price of admission alone. It houses a dazzling display of turquoise tiles from Limoges.

Water, water everywhere

Watery Ghent has always craved a passageway to the sea, which explains a centuries-old passion for constructing canals. When the Zwin silted up, contributing to the decline of Bruges, the Western Scheldt, between Vlissingen and Antwerp, became the artery for international trade. Charles V gave Ghent permission to create a canal link to the Western Scheldt. When the Scheldt was closed (1648), a new waterway was constructed from Bruges to Ostend, connecting to the Leie via the Coupure system. After the fall of Napoleon, King William I of the Netherlands permitted the creation of the Ghent-Terneuzen sea canal.

Water was used for several important local activities: brewing, dyeing cloth, washing wool, dressing animal skins and soap-making. In recent years, there has been much emphasis on reanimating the waterways by restoring bridges and reopening closed water courses. The Nederschelde is being reopened along the Reep, so the estuary that gave the city its name will be almost completely restored. And there is a swanky new marina near Oude Beestenmarkt, though it's often nearly deserted.

For tourists, the most important waterway is the stretch between Korenlei and Graslei, where you can pick up a boat tour of the city (see p27). The 40-minute historical excursion takes you through the medieval centre, while the 90-minute trip explores much more of the city. Even the basic tour covers sights you're unlikely to trek to on foot: the remnants of the **Prinsenhof**, birthplace of Charles V (it was demolished in the 18th century, and the bricks were used to build factories); and the 15th-century **Rabot**, an imposing double-towered structure that served as a toll gate, a fortified lock and even an ice cellar.

Ghent

North of the historic centre

If you find the south of Ghent too French and fancy, a bit of northern grit should see you right. The impact of the industrial revolution still resonates in the cobbled Patershol, once a workers' slum, now a pastel-painted paean to the joys of gentrification. You can see how it used to be at MIAT, an intriguing museum devoted to industrial architecture; or explore the city's colourful folklore at the Kinderen Alynsgodshuis, where the courtyard café hums with local life on sunny Sundays.

Patershol
Map 3, C3, p254

This waterside warren of narrow cobbled lanes was once home to artisans, leather-workers and, later, magistrates. When industry moved out of town, the area became a notorious slum, full of drinking dens and brothels. Even the police feared venturing in. Over the past two decades, it's been well and truly gentrified, and it's now one of the city's prettiest quarters, packed with restaurants and cottages with colourful window boxes and ochre and amber façades. It's especially lively during the August festival (see p190), when residents set up stalls selling junk, antiques and booze, and Turkish and Spanish music sings out from the terraces of the restaurants on Oudburg. On the final day, a procession of candle-carrying residents in nighties and pyjamas tells the somewhat mournful revellers that the party is finally over.

As for sights, there's **Caermersklooster** (Vrouwebroersstraat 6, T 09-269 2910, www.caermersklooster.be, Tue-Sun 1000-1700, free), a 14th-century monastery and now the Provincial Centre for Art and Cuture. Contemporary art exhibitions and installations are held in the vast white gallery space. It is also a good place to pick up brochures about forthcoming cultural events.

Museum voor Industriële Archeologie en Textiel (MIAT)

Minnemeers 9, **T** 09-269 4200, www.miat.gent.be. *Tue-Sun 1000-1800. €2.50. Map 3, A7, p254*

The intriguing Museum of Industrial Architecture and Textiles, known universally as MIAT, lies on the southern edge of Ghent's 'Turkish Town'. It's a large red-brick building fronted by a garden of plants traditionally used to produce textile dyes. The star exhibit is the spinning jenny smuggled out of England by a local hothead, Lieven Bauwens, in 1800. The acquisition of this technology immediately revived the city's flagging textiles industry, though Bauwens lacked the business nous to make the most of his 'discovery', and ended up bankrupt.

Elsewhere, enlightened exhibitions on industrial history explore the working life of women in textile manufacturing and the exploitation of child labour in the developing world. From the fifth floor, there's a fine view of the hulking Gravensteen and the city spires, rising above a jumble of terracotta and slate-grey roofs. The atmospheric fourth floor has a Tierentyn mustard shopfront, panels from an old café and a huge collection of Dinky toys, among them a Bump and Go car with 'friction mystery action'. There's also a reconstruction of the projection room of an early Ghent cinema, where you can watch old advertisements extolling the virtues of cameras and jams. The museum shop sells old postcards and reproductions of toys and industrial vehicles.

Kinderen Alynsgodshuis

Kraanlei 65, **T** 09-269 2350, www.huisvanalijn.be. *Tue-Sun 1100-1700. €2. Map 3, C4, p254*

Unusually, the Hospice of the Alyn Children owes its existence not to an act of benevolence, but to an act of murder. Back in the 14th century, a feud between the Alyn and Rijm families simmered over in the cathedral, with members of the Alyn family being fatally stabbed during Mass. In penance, the Rijms had to cough up enough cash to create a hospice named in their rivals' memory.

The old almshouses have now been converted into a delightful museum of folklore, set around a pleasant courtyard café that positively throbs with local life on sunny Sunday mornings. Inside, you can learn about daily life in Ghent at the turn of the last century through a series of recreated rooms and shop interiors. There are some fabulously evocative items on display, including a thermometer that runs from 'Senegal' down to 'Moscow 1812'. Most rooms have children's activities, and the temporary displays are refreshingly quirky and light of touch, from a cut-throat razor workshop, dedicated to the perfect shave, to an in-depth exploration of the life of gnomes.

Museum Dr Guislain

Jozef Guislainstraat 43, **T** 09-216 3595, www.museumdrguislain.be. *Tue-Fri 0900-1700, weekends 1300-1700. €5. Trams 1, 10, 11, Guislain stop.*

This fascinating museum is devoted to 'outsider art', works by self-taught artists whose wildly imaginative pictures are often crammed with apocalyptic detail or obsessively repetitive patterns. The collection is housed in Belgium's oldest psychiatric institution, established by Dr Jozef Guislain, who laid the foundations for modern psychiatry.

The sometimes disturbing historical display, with sections on electric shocks and lobotomy, tackles some tough questions – why mad people are restrained, whether exorcism cures insanity and what is 'normal' – and shows how magic, religion, compulsion and science have dealt with insanity and abnormality.

Pass through the courtyard (attractive environments were, according to Guislain, essential for patients' wellbeing) and you will come across residents of the adjacent psychiatric centre wandering around or sitting peacefully on the benches.

De Leiestreek

Follow the River Leie southwest from Ghent and you'll reach one of Flanders's prettiest patches, a sleepy waterside landscape of lush fields and leafy woodland. This is great cycling and picnicking territory, but it's best known for the two artists' colonies who drew inspiration from the region – the first and second schools of Sint-Martens-Latem.

The best starting point is **Deinze**, a 12-minute train ride from Ghent's Sint Pieters station. Pick up brochures and a map from the tourist office in the town hall (Gentpoortstraat 1, **T** 09 381 9501, www.vvvleie streek.be). The **Museum van Deinze en de Leiestreek** (Lucien Matthyslaan 3-5, **T** 09 381 9670, www.museum deinze.be. Tue-Fri 1400-1730, Sat-Sun 1000-1200, 1400-1700. €4) is devoted to the luminaries of the Sint-Martens-Latem schools: look out for Emile Claus's vivid, delicate depiction of youngsters ice-skating in salmony sunlight, Constant Permeke's rugged peasant portraits and Hubert Malfait's study of mounted policemen, which wittily merges the backsides of man and beast.

Then make for **Sint-Martens-Latem** itself, a postcard-perfect ensemble of whitewashed buildings with green shutters and terracotta roofs, scattered around the modest church. Follow the path past the main square towards the river for delightful waterside views and a glimpse of a fairy-tale windmill.

Nearby **Deurle** lacks its neighbour's beauty, but it wins hands down when it comes to culture. Its best museum is the **Museum Dhondt-Dhaenens** (Museumlaan 14, **T** 09 282 5123, www.museumdd.be. Tue-Sun, 1100-1700. €3), a white, low-slung modern structure that's perfectly suited to contemporary art, with classy temporary exhibitions and a collection of canvases by James Ensor, Leon Spilliaert, and the Sint-Martens-Latem crowd.

◉ **Listings**

Antwerp and Ghent museums and galleries

- **Antwerpse Miniatuurstad** Antwerp city history, p83.
- **Bijloke Museum** Ghent city history, p114.
- **Caermersklooster** Contemporary art, p116.
- **De Wereld van Kina** Natural history, p111.
- **Diamant Museum** Diamond science and history, p72.
- **Etnografisch Museum** Ethnography, p44.
- **Extra City** Avant-garde art exhibitions, p89
- **FotoMuseum** Photography, p82.
- **Fort Breendonk** (Willebroek) Nazi history, p96.
- **Gravensteen** Medieval history, p107.
- **Kanaal** (Wijnegem) Art and antiques, p96.
- **Kinderen Alynsgodshuis** Folklore, p117.
- **Koninklijk Museum voor Schone Kunsten** Fine arts, p48.
- **Letterenhuis** Flemish literature, p51.
- **Luchtschipbouw** Panamarenko's artistic inventions, p98.
- **Maagdenhuis** Art and social history, p67.
- **MoMu** Fashion, p56.
- **MUHKA** Contemporary art, p81.
- **Museum aan de Stroom** Maritime history, p90.
- **Museum Dr Guislain** Psychiatry and 'outsider' art, p118.
- **Museum Mayer van den Bergh** Art collection, p66.
- **Museum Plantin-Moretus** 16th-century printing, p54.
- **Museum voor Industriële Archeologie en Textiel (MIAT)** Industrial history and textiles, p117.
- **Museum voor Schone Kunsten** Fine arts, p113.
- **Museum voor Sierkunst** Design through the ages, p108.
- **Nationaal Scheepvartmuseum** Seafaring history, p43.
- **Rockoxhuis** 16th-century domestic life and architecture, p48.
- **Rubenshuis** Rubens' art and life, p62.
- **SMAK** Contemporary art, p112.
- **Vleeshuis** Music, p42.
- **Volkskundemuseum** Folk history, p38.

Sleeping

As you'd expect in a thriving commercial city, Antwerp's hoteliers rely on business travellers, not tourists, so there are fewer characterful central hotels than you might hope for, and the boutiques tend to be booked up well in advance. But that shouldn't stop you staying in style, as the city is blessed with dozens of brilliant B&Bs: some are sleek, space-age shrines to contemporary design, others unashamed olde-worlde romantics, and many offer astounding value for money. The corporate hotels tend to slash prices at weekends and at the last minute, which might make them worth considering (www.bookings.be is a good place to look). Ghent has several good hotels, but no stunners, and a smattering of spectacular B&Bs; again, look out for weekend deals. If you're planning to go for the Gentse Feesten, book way in advance; go afterwards, and hotels are almost giving rooms away.

For more accommodation listings, visit www.gastenkamersantwerpen.be, www.weekend hotel.nl, www.bedandbreakfast-gent.be or www.bedandbreakfast.com/belgium.

Sleeping codes

Historic centre

Hotels

LL De Witte Lelie, Keizerstraat 16-18, **T** 03-226 1966, www.dewittelelie.be. *Map 2, C7, p253* If money is no object, or if you're seeking to impress, the White Lily is the only place to be. The 10 rooms are housed in three 17th-century town houses with whitewashed, step-gabled façades. They are light, airy and jaw-droppingly gorgeous, their period features enhanced by crisp white linen, cool marble and unobtrusive modern touches. Add in the tranquil courtyard and breakfast in bed, and it's no surprise that you need to book weeks in advance.

L Julien, Korte Nieuwstraat 24, **T** 03-229 0600, www.hotel-julien.com. *Map 2, C6, p252* For once, a design hotel that doesn't think friendly service is uncool. A pinky-green light glows in the high-ceilinged hallway, the beige and cream rooms are calm and understated, with top-quality fabrics, and breakfast is served on specially commissioned ceramics in a beautiful black and white room with gorgeous original features. But it's the staff's attitude – or lack of it – that makes a stay here so special.

L 't Sandt, Het Zand 17-19, **T** 03-232 9390, www.hotel-sandt.be. *Map 2, D3, p252* This elegant town-house hotel near Sint-Jansvliet sets high standards for itself, with suites named after legendary hotels such as the Ritz, the Raffles and the Negresco. There's certainly an air of discreet luxury in the shiny lobby, with black and white tiles and flowers everywhere. Many of the cosy rooms have balconies or terraces; all have firm beds and light, bright decor. Splash out on the beamed Cathedral Penthouse, where you can soak up views of that iconic spire from the bathtub.

A Hotel Prinse, Keizerstraat 63, **T** 03-226 4050, www.hotel prinse.be. *Map 2, C8, p253* On the same street as the Witte Lelie, but a tad further from the Grote Markt, this friendly hotel has a slightly corporate feel, but the cobbled inner courtyard lends it considerable charm, and the brown and grey decor is refreshingly unfussy. Free internet access in the lobby.

A Rubens Grote Markt, Oude Beurs 29, **T** 03-222 4848, www.hotelrubensantwerp.be. *Map 2, B5, p252* Top marks for the quiet central location, in a building with the oldest tower in Antwerp, but be warned: the decor, with floral prints and fox-hunting pictures to the fore, veers dangerously close to kitsch. The vast Rubens suite (€445) has a private garden. Parking available: €15 per day.

C Hotel Antigone, Jordaenskaai 11/12, **T** 03-231 6677, www.antigonehotel.be. *Map 2, A4, p252* Antwerp's only riverside hotel is a short walk from the Grote Markt. It's not the swishest place in town, but the high-ceilinged, brightly coloured rooms offer good value. If you want a view, ask for a top-floor room – but riverside means roadside, so those rooms can be noisy. Add €10 if you want a bath rather than a shower.

C Wake Up Studio, Hoogstraat 68, **T** 03-225 1606, www.antigone hotel.be. *Map 2, D3, p252* If you don't care about hotel services, this is an excellent central option, on a bustling street between the Grote Markt and Sint-Jansvliet. The cosy studio apartments are simple, with light wood, white furnishings and kitchenettes.

D Postiljon, Blauwmoezelstraat 6, **T** 03-231 7575. *Map 2, C5, p252* In the shadow of the cathedral, this old inn has had a much-needed makeover, and is now a cheap and cheerful family-run affair. The smallish, simple rooms, some with shared facilities, are brightened up by coloured glass windowpanes. Great situation for late-night pub crawls, if your head can take the morning bells.

D Scheldezicht, Sint-Jansvliet 10-12, **T** 03-231 6602, www.hotel-scheldezicht.be. *Map 2, D3, p252* Eccentric establishment on a characterful square near the river. The rooms (most with showers) are slightly down at heel but spacious and full of charm. Breakfast is served in a cluttered room from which you can pop out to the antiques market on Sunday.

B&Bs

A-B The Grace, Lange Nieuwstraat 25, **T** 03-234 9148. *Map 2, D6, p252* Not far from lovely Conscienceplein, this artfully designed B&B offers two rooms, the spacious 'Grey' and the more expensive 'Master' bedroom (€150), an en suite mezzanine with a rooftop terrace. The owner is often away, so guests get the run of the stylish living room and adjacent terrace. If you fancy champagne and caviar for breakfast, you need only ask.

C Guesthouse 26, Pelgrimstraat 26, **T** 0497-428369, www.guesthouse26.com. *Map 2, D4, p252* A delightful place in a 19th-century town house on one of the city's prettiest streets. The public areas are pleasantly cluttered with curios, and you can choose between baroque, oriental, 1960s and 'old English' rooms, some with en suite facilities. There's free parking five minutes away.

D Emperor's 48, Keizerstraat 48, **T** 03-228 7337, www.emperors 48.com. *Map 2, C7, p253* A friendly B&B near the Rockoxhuis, with two simple rooms that can easily sleep three. The decor is simple but stylish, with warm wooden floors and a blue and red colour scheme. All guests have access to the pretty, south-facing roof terrace. There's a €10 reduction if you stay during the week.

D-E Bousard-Rodriguez, Sudermanstraat 18, **T** 0485-133449, www.bousardrodriguez.com. *Map 2, D6, p252* This hospitable B&B offers two simple rooms with TVs, CD players and private bathrooms in the main house, built in 1910. Around the corner, next to the neo-Gothic stock exchange, is a lovely apartment with living room, kitchenette, modern bathroom and upstairs double bedroom, great value at €80 per night.

Sint-Andries and the Latin Quarter

Hotels

L Theater Hotel, Arenbergstraat 30, **T** 03-203-5410, www.vhv-hotels.be. *Map 2, F7, p253* Though it's aimed at a business clientele, this elegant establishment near the Bourla theatre has plenty of character, with spacious, classy-looking rooms and attractive public spaces. Guests get free use of the wooden sauna.

B 't Elzenveld, Lange Gasthuisstraat 45, **T** 03-202 7707, www.elzenveld.be. *Map 2, G6, p252* Near the Mayer van den Bergh Museum and the Botanical Gardens, this is essentially a conference centre – but don't let that put you off. The peaceful, often beamed rooms in this medieval hospital complex are arranged around a pretty courtyard and the adjacent chapel hosts classical music concerts.

C Cammerpoorte, Nationalestraat 38-40, **T** 03-231 9736, www.hotelcammerpoorte.be. *Map 2, E4, p252* A small, unfussy hotel in the heart of the fashion district, with simple modern rooms and a private car park.

Diamond and Jewish districts

Hotels

L Alfa De Keyser, De Keyserlei 66-70, **T** 03-206 7460, www.vhv-hotels.be. *Map 2, E12, p253* Part of the upmarket Alfa chain, this hotel near Centraal station has smart, spacious rooms with the usual businessman-friendly facilities. There's a good fitness centre with sauna, hot tub and solarium.

L Alfa Empire, Appelmansstraat 31, **T** 03-203 5400, www.vhv-hotels.be. *Map 2, E11, p253* Another member of the Alfa chain, the Empire is an efficient, business-oriented hotel, but not without style. It's cheaper than its sisters, but the rooms are simpler and a little smaller.

L Astrid Park Plaza, Koningin Astridplein 7, **T** 03-203 1234, www.parkplaza.com. *Map 2, D12, p253* This efficient, twin-turreted modern hotel, with post-modern architecture that echoes Centraal station, has good-sized, comfortable rooms and a decent fitness centre, with a gym, pool, hot tub and sauna.

L Hyllit, De Keyserlei 28-30, **T** 03-202 6800, www.hyllithotel.be. *Map 2, E11, p253* More modern than the nearby De Keyser, but just as friendly and efficient, the Hyllit lies behind a vast white and glass façade. The large rooms have a grey colour scheme that's a good deal less dreary than you might expect, and it trumps its rivals in the fitness-centre stakes, thanks to a Turkish bath.

B Colombus, Frankrijklei 4, **T** 03-233 0390, www.colombushotel. com. *Map 2, E10, p253* A friendly, family-run establishment near the opera house, with an attractive art nouveau breakfast room, a cosy lounge with piano, a fitness room, a pool and artwork with a musical theme. The simply furnished rooms vary hugely in size – ask for a quiet one, away from the main road. It's worth haggling for a last-minute deal.

Hostels

E-G New International Youth Hotel, Provinciestraat 256, **T** 03-230 0522, www.youthhotel.be. *Map 1, F8, p251* Not far from the Zurenborg, this family-friendly hostel (children under seven stay free) has dormitory beds (€19.50) and rooms sleeping two or four. Some even have en suite bathrooms (a double with shower costs €58). Breakfast is included. WiFi access, but no kitchen.

G Boomerang Youth Hostel, Lange Leemstraat 95-97, **T** 03-238 4782, www.boomeranghostel.be. *Map 1, F5, p250* Smart, cosy hostel in a former school south of the Stadspark, a 15-minute tram ride from the centre. Dormitory beds €12, twins €30, buffet breakfast €2.50.

Het Zuid

Hotels

L-A Slapen Enzo, Karel Rogierstraat 20, **T** 03-216 2785, www.slapenenzo.be. *Map 1, F2, p250* This super-stylish boutique hotel (the name means 'To sleep, and then...') has six rooms in various minimalist permutations of black and white. It takes itself a little seriously – the first heading on the website is 'philosophy', and there's a sculpture patio – but the quality of the linen and bathroom products is beyond reproach, and rooms come with flatscreen TVs, sound systems, WiFi and, in the pricier Living Room, a double jacuzzi.

C Industrie, Emiel Banningstraat 52, **T** 03-238 8660, www.hotelindustrie.be. *Map 1, G1, p250* A small, hospitable guesthouse near the Justitiepaleis, decorated throughout in mock-Parisian style, with floral fabrics and Toulouse-Lautrec posters on the wall. The cheaper rooms are on the sardine side of cosy, but easy to fall into after a night on the tiles, and you'll find leaflets and brochures on all the local attractions in the lobby.

D Rubenshof, Amerikalei 115-117, **T** 03-237 0789, www.rubens hof.be. *Map 1, F3, p250* You'll get good value for your money at this friendly hotel in a 19th-century town house on the Zuid's northeastern fringe; doubles with shared facilities start at just €40. The rooms don't live up to the elegant public areas – all stained glass and stucco – but they're simple, tasteful and comfortable. It has plenty of fans, so book well in advance.

B&Bs

L Charles Rogier XI, Karel Rogierstraat 11, **T** 0475-299989, www.charlesrogierXI.be. *Map 1, F2, p250* If posey minimalist hotels leave you cold, try this unabashedly opulent boutique B&B, the self-styled 'Queen Mum of all Antwerp private guesthouses'. With four-poster beds, antiques, boldly striped and tartanned wallpaper, comfy armchairs and paintings of enigmatic-looking ladies, the dimly lit, deeply romantic rooms make you wonder what the pre-Raphaelites would have been like if they'd had a sense of humour. The Lady of the House, Katrin S'Jongers, certainly does – but she also has impeccable taste and a flair for making her guests feel at home.

B Patine, Leopold de Waelstraat 1, **T** 03-257 0919, www.guesthouses.be. *Map 1, F1, p250* There's only one room above this popular wine bar, but what a room it is: warm wooden floor, cosy rugs, old-fashioned green lampshades, a sofa bed for extra guests, art books aplenty, a fridge and views of the Fine Arts Museum.

E Bed, Bad, Brood, Justitiestraat 43, **T** 03-248 1539. *Map 1, F4, p250* From the monumental, high-ceilinged hallway onwards, everything here is big. Even the 'small' room, with a bathroom across the corridor, is a decent size (and a bargain at €40). The top-floor studio (€55) has a pretty blue-green bathroom and cooking facilities. Breakfast is served in the winter garden, overlooking grape-bearing vines. The owners have small children, and welcome families.

F Ann, Paul and Kids, Verschansingstraat 55, **T** 03-248 0913, www.bbantwerp.be. *Map 1, F1, p250* Handily placed between the Fine Arts Museum and the Waalse Kaai, this is a charmingly informal, unpolished B&B. The owners have small children, and see young families as a potential source of playmates; grown-ups can join Ann's yoga classes for free.

Youth hostels

G Op Sinjoorke, Eric Sasselaan 2, **T** 03-238 0273, www.vjh.be. *Map 1, off H5 (off map), p250* Just outside the ring, this large hostel has good facilities (kitchen, parking, nearby bus and tram stops).

G Sleep Inn, Bolivarplaats 1, **T** 03-237 3748. *Map 1, off G1, p250* Small hostel with basic rooms and studios in the deep south of the Zuid, near the new law courts. TV room and kitchen.

Voegelzang Camping Ground, Vogelzanglaan 7-9, **T** 03-238 5117. *Map 1, off H5 (off map), p250* Two hikers' cabins.

't Eilandje

B&Bs

D Hotelit, Extra City, Mexicostraat, **T** 0484-421070, www.extra city.org. *Map 1, A11, p251* Run by Extra City, a contemporary-art gallery (see p89), this is not so much a hotel room as an art installation. Your heart will sink on seeing what looks like a shipping container, but step inside and you'll be transported by the glass wall overlooking the Kattendijkdok and the city beyond. The walls are covered with paintings and drawings, and exhibitionists can leave the curtains open, so passers-by can peep inside. Guests get free admission to Extra City, and somewhere to stagger back to after a session at the Fake Bar (see p168).

D Logies Diamond Princess, Bonapartedok, St-Laureiskaai 1, **T** 03-227 0815. *Map 1, off A3, p250* You don't need sea legs to stay on this former cruise ship in the heart of the Eilandje's action. The rooms are basic, and decorated in neutral colours, but there is something undeniably romantic about gazing through your porthole window at the rippling waters of the dock.

Camping

De Molen, Sint-Annastrand, Thonetlaan, **T** 03-219 8179. *Apr-Sep. Map 1, off A1 (off map), p250* A pitch at this Left Bank camping ground near Sint-Anneke beach costs €1.25, then €2.50 per person, and comes with free views of the city skyline. Electricity costs €1.25. Log cabins and a four-person chalet are also available.

Zurenborg

B&Bs

A La Rimessa, Lamorinièrestraat 127, **T** 03-286 7098,
www.larimessa.be. *Map 1, H7, p251* The modest façade of this
town house hardly prepares you for the splendour inside. There is
just one stunning, spacious suite, in pretty mint and terracotta
shades, with a private balcony, a beautifully decorated bathroom, a
flatscreen TV and cashmere covers on the bed. Breakfast is served
in an elegant ground-floor veranda with views of the vast, lush
garden, and you don't have to worry about losing the keys: they
have a fingerprint-recognition system.

F Mabuhay, Draakstraat 32, **T** 03-290 8815, www.mabuhay.be.
Map 1, G9, p251 A modest house with smallish rooms near Cogels-
Osylei. The largest room has its own toilet; otherwise, you share
with the owners and residents.

Borgerhout

B&Bs

C Ecohuis, Turnhoutsebaan 13, **T** 03-217 0811, www.eha.be.
Map 1, D10, p251 Above the sustainable show flat at the Ecohuis is
a wooden-floored duplex apartment that can easily accommodate
four, with a kitchen, a dining room and a private balcony. You get
one night free if you stay for three – and a satisfying sense that
you're saving the planet.

E Het Melkhuis, Groenstraat 25, **T** 03-272 5539. *Map 1, D9,
p251* A bright, eco-friendly B&B in a former dairy, 10 minutes' walk

from Centraal station, with two simple, freshly decorated rooms. Guests are treated as part of the family, and can lounge in the lovely rambling garden.

Ghent

Hotels

L Novotel, Goudenleeuwplein 5, **T** 09-224 2230, www.novotel.com. *Map 3, F4, p254* Yes, it's a chain hotel, but a comfortable one, and in a brilliant position near the cathedral. There's a garden with an outdoor pool, so you can have a quick dip before strolling off to see the Lamb of God. Sauna, fitness centre, and private parking available.

L-A St Jorishof, Botermarkt 2, **T** 09-224 2424, www.courst georges.com. *Map 3, F4, p254* Founded in 1228, the step-gabled St Jorishof claims to be Europe's oldest hotel, with Charles V and Napoleon among the celebrity guests. Nowadays, it's a Best Western, and you sleep in an 18th-century town house across the road. Which is a bit of an anticlimax, to be honest, though the rooms have a bright, contemporary feel.

A Hotel De Flandre, Poel 1-2, **T** 09-266 0600, www.hotelde flandre.be. *Map 3, F1, p254* A new hotel with a bit of history: there was a guesthouse here from the 18th century, and Johann Strauss once stayed. Bay trees, fountains and stone troughs decorate the terrace courtyard; the lounge has chairs tastefully cloaked in grey; and the rooms are kitted out in quiet browns and greys, with beams on the top floor, once the servants' quarters.

A Ghent River Hotel, Waaistraat 5, **T** 09-266 1010, www.ghent-river-hotel.be. *Map 3, D2, p254* Just off the Vrijdagmarkt, and backing onto, yes, the river, this building is a blend of a 16th-century house and a 19th-century rice mill, with a modern façade for good measure. The best rooms are in the old bit, with exposed beams or bricks; otherwise, you get plenty of space, wooden floors, cream walls, dark brown furniture and large, comfy beds. The top-floor breakfast room is a wonderfully light place to start the day, with spire and belfry views an added bonus.

A Hotel Gravensteen, Jan Breydelstraat 35, **T** 09-225 1150, www.gravensteen.be. *Map 3, D2, p254* An elegant, smoothly run establishment in a striking grey-stone building on one of the city's most atmospheric streets. A winding staircase leads up from the marble lobby to rooms that are comfortable, if somewhat conventional. Fitness centre, sauna, bike rental.

A Hotel Harmony, Kraanlei 37, **T** 09-324 2680, www.hotel-harmony.be. *Map 3, C3, p254* A stylish new boutique hotel in the Patershol, with views of the city's three towers. There's a warm, contemporary feel to the decor, with big, comfy beds and colourful fabrics, and some rooms have modern four-posters; you can also rent a studio with kitchenette.

A-B Boatel, Voorhoutkaai 29A, **T** 09-267 1030, www.the boatel.com. *Map 3, off G8 (off map), p255* In the new Portus Ganda harbour, east of the city centre, this converted 1950s boat offers five bright modern rooms with chic tiled shower rooms in the old cargo hold and two more spacious 'luxury rooms' (€130).

A-C Poortackere Monasterium, Oude Houtlei 56, **T** 09-269 2210, www.monasterium.be. *Map 3, I1, p255* Once a convent, this atmospheric, vaulted neo-Gothic complex now has colourful en suite rooms in the main hotel and simpler guesthouse accommodation in the authentically austere nuns' former cells. Breakfast is served in the chapter house or the delightful garden.

B-C Erasmus, Poel 25 **T** 09-224 2195, www.erasmushotel.be. *Map 3, F1, p254* A delightfully old-fashioned hotel in a twin-gabled, 16th-century patrician house, near the Museum voor Sierkunst. The decor is hardly cutting-edge, but the attic rooms have authentic beamed ceilings, and the whole place has bags of character. Have an early-evening drink in the formal garden, with gravelled paths and a patio terrace, and pop into the sitting room for a peek at the owner's organ.

D Brooderie, Jan Breydelstraat 8, **T** 09-225 0623. *Map 3, E2, p254* This waterside establishment near the pretty Grashrug has three simple, cosy upstairs rooms (two doubles, one single) with wooden floors and furniture. Breakfast is served in the downstairs bakery.

F Flandria Centrum, Barrestraat 3, **T** 09-223 0626, www.flandria-centrum.be. *Map 3, G7, p255* Characterful, family-run budget hotel on a quiet street near the cathedral, with simple, affordable rooms done out in upbeat pinks and reds and a cheerfully cluttered feel. Exceptional value.

B&Bs

B Engelen aan de Waterkant, Ter Platen 30, **T** 09-223 0883, www.engelenaandewaterkant.be. *Map 3, off L7 (off map), p255* A 25-minute walk from the cathedral, the canalside "Angels on the Waterfront" is utterly divine. The owner, Ann Willems, runs the design boutique on the ground floor, and she's brought all her know-how to the two vast rooms: filled with tubs of fabric roses, they have white-wood floors and sumptuous bathrooms with chandeliers.

B-C Verzameld Werk, Onderstraat 23, **T** 09-224 2712, www.verzameldwerk.be. *Map 3, D4, p254* Owned by the next-door design studio, this modernized 14th-century house offers a white-walled suite and two duplexes that mix period features with furniture by stylemongers such as Jasper Morrison and Arne Jacobsen. Many of the fixtures are multifunctional – there's a spacehopper-style white light that you can sit on or eat off, and the coat hooks are actually plates. If you like it, make your mark on the 'guestbook' – a kitchen worksurface-cum-blackboard on which you draw your impressions in chalk.

D Chambre Plus, Hoogpoort 31, **T** 09-225 3775, www.chambreplus.be. *Map 3, E4, p254* This central, hospitable B&B has two en suite rooms – the Congo, with cool mock-colonial decor and fabrics, and the more flamboyant Sultan – and a superb duplex beyond the pretty courtyard at the back of the house, the Côte Sud (€140), with a hot tub from which you can gaze at the stars, thanks to the skylight above.

D Folklore, Lange Steenstraat 69, **T** 09-224 3118, **T** 0475-265660. *Map 3, A3, p254* If it's authenticity you're after, how about staying at one of the city's most traditional pubs, in the Patershol neighbourhood? You cross a courtyard behind the bar to reach the simply furnished duplex studio, which has two double beds and a kitchenette. Breakfast is €7.50.

Youth hostels

G De Draecke, Sint-Widostraat 11, **T** 09-233 7050. *Map 3, C2, p254* A highly superior hostel, with neat, clean rooms in a gorgeous canalside location.

Eating and drinking

If you can judge something's significance by the number of words used to describe it, then eating out is clearly vital for every Antwerpenaar. Restaurant, café, bar, bistro, brasserie, *eetcafé*, *praatcafé*, *estaminet*, *bistrant*… trying to work out the difference can be bewildering. The simplest option is not to bother: the British distinction between restaurants, bars and cafés simply doesn't exist here, and there are scores of places where you can go for coffee, a beer, a light lunch or a full-blown dinner. It's almost impossible to have a bad meal in Antwerp, where intense competition for customers has led to stratospheric standards of cooking. Restaurants are not cheap, but they offer serious value for money, and portions are usually huge. For those on a budget, most cafés and brasseries offer omelettes and croques alongside the pricier dishes. Restaurants generally serve meals from 1200-1430 and 1830- 2300; snacks are available all day. Many only have menus in Dutch (you're more likely to see French and English versions in Ghent). Non-smoking areas are not common, but a ban on smoking in restaurants should come into force in 2007.

Eating codes

Price		
ᵼᵼᵼ	€35 and over
ᵼᵼ	€20–€35
ᵼ	€20 and under

Prices refer to the cost of a two-course meal without drinks.

During the First World War, the story goes, a British officer heard French-speaking soldiers talking about *frites* and concluded that they were a French invention, hence 'French fries'. Wrong. Those soldiers were Belgian, and Belgium is mighty proud of its chips, double-fried for perfect crispiness and usually scoffed with mayonnaise. The tradition goes back centuries: the first potato recipes were written by a Belgian, Lancelot de Casteau, in 1604.

Chips are not the only national speciality worth seeking out: signature Belgian dishes include the inevitable mussels (though these often come from Holland), unctuous shrimp croquettes, eel in a herby 'green' sauce, *stoofvlees* (beef stewed to tender perfection in beer), rabbit cooked in cherry beer, plump white asparagus (May-June), prawn-stuffed tomatoes and chicory and ham gratiné.

There's also a distinct Flemish cuisine: there's *stoemp* (sausage and mash) or *hutsepot* (meat hotpot, with turnips, spice and herbs). Antwerp offers sausage and apple breads, raisin breads and *handjes* (hand-shaped biscuits and chocolates with marzipan filling); Ghent, meanwhile, weighs in with *waterzooï* (a creamy fish or chicken stew with vegetables), cured Ganda ham, *stoverij* (a beef and offal stew), spicy Tierenteyn mustard (made to a secret recipe brought from Dijon by exiles during the Napoleonic era) and *mastellas* (rolled-up pastry with cinnamon and brown sugar). A more recent Ghent invention is the Martino sandwich, which is basically steak tartare with capers, onion – and mindblowing quantities of Tabasco.

Historic centre

Restaurants

€€€ Bernardin, Sint-Jakobsstraat 17, **T** 03-213 0700, www.restaurantbernardin.be. *Map 2, C8, p253 Tue-Fri 1200-1430, 1830-2230, Sat dinner only, Sun-Mon lunch only*. A handsome town house east of the cathedral, with a swish white interior and a dreamy terrace in the shadow of Sint-Jacob's church. The cooking is top-notch modern French: heavenly foie gras, duck confit and papillote of baked langoustines. Service is formal but impeccable.

€€€ De Kleine Zavel, Stoofstraat 2, **T** 03-231 9691. *Sun-Fri 1200-1400, 1800-2230, Fri-Sat 1830-2300. Map 2, D3, p252* A long-time local favourite, serving fusion cuisine in a baroque-meets-brasserie setting with crates of empty wine bottles stacked between the tables. Imaginative fish and seafood dishes are the speciality – cannelloni of tuna and lobster tempura, sea bass with king crab *loempia* – and the 'four-ways tuna' is divine.

€€€ Gin-Fish, Haarstraat 9, **T** 03-231 3207. *Wed-Sat 1800-2200, Tue 1200-1400, 1800-2200. Map 2, C3, p252* If you want to know exactly what's going onto your plate – or if you fancy the finest, freshest fish dishes in town – take a bar stool by the stainless-steel counter that surrounds Didier Garnich's open kitchen and watch as he whips up supper before your eyes. There's no menu, just four fabulous courses (€75, with wine) comprising whatever took the chef's fancy at market that morning, but you're firmly in lobster and turbot territory here.

€€€ Rucolla, Wolstraat 45, **T** 03-231 8994, www.larucolla.be. *1200-1400, closed Wed, Sun. Map 2, C6, p252* Off Conscienceplein, this sleek, stylish restaurant with chocolate walls and black and

Eating

white photographs offers creative Franco-Italian cuisine: scallop tartare; steak with foie gras, caramelized chicory, truffle purée and port sauce; veal with wild mushrooms and herbs; baked turbot with lemongrass. This is a labour of love, and it shows, especially in the service. On weekdays, lunch is a steal at €18.50.

€€€ **Sir Anthony van Dijck**, Vlaeykensgang, Oude Koornmarkt 16, **T** 03-231 6170, www.siranthonyvandijck.be. *Mon-Sat 1200-1400, 1830-late. Map 2, C4, p252* Marc Paesbrugghe is a Red Guide refusenik, who surrendered his Michelin star because his culinary vision clashed with the strict criteria. That hasn't stopped tourists and loyal locals from flocking to this sumptuous restaurant in the city's prettiest alley for millefeuille of freshwater lobster, poached cod with olive purée or veal medallions with peppers and artichoke.

€€ **Brasserie Appelmans**, Papenstraatje 1, **T** 03-226 2022, www.brasserieappelmans.be. *1130-2300. Map 2, D4, p252* A standout amid the tacky joints near the cathedral, with cavernous ceilings, a black colour scheme and warmly lit brick walls. The food is Belgian with a contemporary twist – shrimp croquettes with sweet pepper sauce, tempura of Belgian cheeses with fresh figs – and the club-style sandwiches make a perfect light-ish lunch.

€€ **De 7 Schaken**, Braderijstraat 24, **T** 03-232 5244. *Daily 1100-0300, kitchen from 1100-2300. Map 2, B4, p252* This cosy, wood-panelled tavern is named after the city's seven 'founding families', and the food and decor are suitably traditional. The steaks, *stoemp* and shrimp croquettes are enormous, while stews come in a seemingly bottomless pot. It hums with chat at lunch, and is a great spot to hear the summer carillon concerts.

€€ **Dock's Café**, Jordaenskaai 7, **T** 03-226 6330, www.docks.be. *Daily 1200-1430, 1800-2300, Fri -2400, Sat 1800-2400, Sun 1200-2230. Map 2, A3, p252* With a theatrical wood-and-iron ship-style interior,

Eating

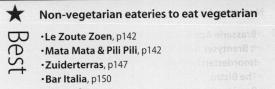

this is a typically flamboyant offering from the Belgian restaurant guru Antonio Pinto. The food is French and Italian, with fish and seafood the stars (there's also an oyster bar). Lunch €15.

€€ Le Zoute Zoen, Zirkstraat 15-17, **T** 03-226 9220. *Tue-Thu 1200-1500, 1800-2200, Fri-Sat -2300. No lunch Sat. Map 2, B5, p252* Delightful bistro with wax-caked candelabras, a mosaic floor and cluttered bookshelves. It looks more formal than it is, and therein lies its charm. Background music ranges from drum'n'bass to smoky jazz. The food is Belgo-French with an Italian twist, and extremely accomplished: try scallops in truffle sauce.

€€ Mata Mata & Pili Pili, Hoogstraat 44, **T** 03-213 1928, www.matamatapilipili.be. *1800-2230. Map 2, D3, p252* Get a taste of Africa – Congolese chicken moambe, Nigerian beef stew with peanut sauce and a variety of fish curries – in a cheery setting with black and white check decor, masks and coconut shells on the walls and a lime-green cocktail bar.

€€ Noord, Grote Markt 24, **T** 03-232 8216. *Mon-Sat 0900-0300. Map 2, C4, p252* For a drink or meal in the shadow of Silvius Brabo, you won't better this bustling, thoroughly Belgian brasserie with a sprawling terrace, a heated winter garden and super-efficient waiters. Stick to the staples: prawncroquettes, beef in beer, shrimp-stuffed tomatoes and a Trappist ale or three.

★ **Non-stop kitchens**

Best

- **Brasserie Appelmans**, p141
- **'t Brantyser**, 143
- **Noorderterras**, p143
- **The Bistro**, p146
- **Bassin**, p153

€€ **Noorderterras**, Jordaenskaai 27, **T** 03-290 0857, www.noorderterras.be. *Daily 1100-2300. Map 2, C6, p252* Relaxed, atmospheric eetcafé with leather banquettes, warm crimson drapes and delightful river views. The menu spans sauce-drenched steaks and smaller snacks (crostini with white truffle and goat's cheese, vegetable spring rolls with aubergine caviar). Children may faint over the *dame blanche*, beautifully presented with separate pots of whipped cream and hot chocolate sauce.

€€ **'t Brantyser**, Hendrik Conscienceplein 7, **T** 03-233 1833, www.brantyser.be. *Tavern 1115-1700, weekends 1100-late, restaurant 1700-late. Map 2, C6, p252* A classic tavern on the city's classiest square, with beamed ceilings, chandeliers, a tiled floor and a terrace next to Carolus Borromeo church. No-nonsense Belgian fare – steak, mussels, North Sea sole, shoulder of lamb and generous salads – and wok dishes. Daily special €9.30.

€€ **'t Stil Genieten**, Sint-Nicolaasplaats 10, **T** 03-213 0282. *Tue-Sun, Sat evenings only. Map 2, C8, p253* With a terrace on a medieval courtyard, this is a great spot for an indulgent lunch with a side order of streaky bacon. The cooking is refined Belgo-French: lamb fillet with rosemary potatoes and aubergine tartlet, bouillabaisse and monkfish with curry sauce.

Eating

€ **Façade**, Hendrik Conscienceplein 18, **T** 03-233 5931. *Mon-Fri 1030-2230, Sat-Sun 1100-2330. Map 2, C6, p252* Good-value brasserie – omelette, steaks, pasta – with neat neo-Seventies decor and a penchant for extravagant side salads.

€ **Sjalot en Schanul**, Oude Beurs 12, **T** 03-233 8875. *Mon-Fri 1000-2000, Sat-Sun 1000-0200. Map 2, B4, p252* Small, friendly eatery with warm orange walls and baskets laden with vegetables and pumpkins on the window sills. The excellent salads, sandwiches, toasts and pastas are made with organic produce. Snap up a jar of homemade jam before you leave.

€ **'t Hofke**, Vlaeykensgang, Oude Koornmarkt 16, **T** 03-233 8606. *Mon-Fri 1200-1500 and 1800-late, Sat-Sun 1200-late. Map 2, C4, p252* An informal lunch venue and tearoom with a delightful terrace, where you dine at tables decorated with fresh flowers beneath vines and a fig tree. Try basil-flavoured bread with homemade pesto, tagliatelle with prawns and cognac sauce or the soup of the day, great value at just €4.

Cafés

In de Gloria, Kleine Koraalberg 8, **T** 03-232 5908. *Mon, Wed-Sun 1100-0300. Map 2, B4, p252* Good old Flemish cooking (stews and *stoemp*) in an atmospheric building that dates back to 1600. In fine weather, the pretty terrace is a good spot for listening to carillon concerts.

Via Via Reiscafé, Wolstraat 43, **T** 03-226 4749. *Mon-Fri 1130-0100, Sat-Sun 1230-0200. Map 2, C6, p252* Part of a small worldwide chain that tries to bring tourists and locals together, Via Via serves inexpensive dishes from around the world, so you can opt for a frugal feta sandwich or some tandoori chicken as you leaf through a dog-eared guidebook from the café's travel library.

Sint-Andries and the Latin Quarter

Restaurants

€€€ **Hecker**, Kloosterstraat 13, **T** 03-234 3834, www.hecker.be. *Mon from 1800, Tue, Thu-Sun from 1000.* Map 2, F2, p252 The dining room of this restaurant-cum-wine bar has exposed piping, chocolate-coloured walls and large windows through which you can size up the stock in the nearby antiques shop. The food is fabulous – seafood ravioli, octopus carpaccio, cod in coconut cappuccino or grilled lobster with smoked garlic – and there's a well-judged wine list, with 12-15 vintages by the glass. Four-course 'menu surprise' €48, business lunch €17.

€€€ **Het Nieuwe Palinghuis**, Sint-Jansvliet 14, **T** 03-231 7445, www.hetnieuwepalinghuis.be. *Wed-Sun 1200-1500, 1800-2200. Map 2, D3, p252* The New Eel House is in fact something of an institution, with a formal feel, appropriately nostalgic photographs of Antwerp and decades of expertise to recommend it. Fish is the thing here: salad of grilled scallops, bouillabaisse, fried eel, lobster with mushrooms, or sea bass in a salt crust.

€€€ **Huis de Colvenier**, Sint-Antoniusstraat 8, **T** 03-226 6573, www.colvenier.be. *Mon-Sat 1200-1500, 1900-2200. Map 2, F4, p252* Housed in a 19th-century patrician town house with chandeliers and stuccoed cream walls, the Colvenier feels like a private dining room, with waiters flamboyantly whisking the covers off silver tureens. This is one of the city's finest restaurants, and the French-influenced food is out of this world: lobster with tomato chutney, lamb with Meaux mustard and a Savoy cabbage hotpot, roast wood pigeon with foie gras and a sauce made with truffle and veal jus. If you can't decide, try the seven-course 'discovery' menu (€100, including wines).

€€ **Berlin**, Kleine Markt 1-3, **T** 03-227 1101. *Mon-Fri 0730-late, Sat-Sun 1000-late. Map 2, F5, p252* It's a tough task being trendy and child-friendly at the same time, but this lively bar-café-restaurant pulls it off with aplomb. Its secret weapon is a playroom out back. There's a buzz at all hours, and you can tarry over tapas or get stuck into marinated ribs, veal steak with a truffle and lemon sauce or salmon lasagne. The service is a little erratic, but then, dodging tricycles probably wasn't in the job description.

€€ **The Bistro**, Wapper 1A, **T** 03-232 3675, www.thebistro.be. *1100-1000. Map 2, E8, p253* Proximity to the Rubenshuis is not the only reason this cosy brasserie attracts the crowds. Fans of correct service and classic Flemish and Belgian dishes flock here for beer-stewed rabbit with prunes, duck in kriek, succulent steaks or chicken waterzooï. Parents, meanwhile, will appreciate the children's menu and the terrace on the pedestrianized Wapper.

€€ **Bourla/Mares**, Kelderstraat 2, **T** 03-226 3033. *Mon-Sat 1200-1500, 1800-2300. Map 2, F7, p253* A stone's throw from the Bourla theatre, and especially popular for lunch, this cheerful, upbeat eatery with green walls and a giant chandelier serves straightforward salads, pasta and excellent shrimp croquettes.

€€ **De Foyer**, Komedieplaats 48, **T** 03-233 5517, www.defoyer.be. *Mon-Sat 1100-2400, Sun 1100-1800 (brunch 1400-). Map 2, F7, p253* Beneath a resplendent painted rotunda, the brasserie of the Bourla theatre (see p68) is a glorious place with everything as it should be: red curtains, green marble tables, extravagant ferns, brass chandeliers, mirrors and the busy clink of cutlery. Even a coffee comes with a sense of occasion. Sunday brunch here is an Antwerp institution, and must be booked at least three weeks in advance.

€€ **Horta**, Hopland 2, **T** 03-232 2815, www.grandcafehorta.be. *0900-2300, Fri-Sat -2400. Map 2, F8, p253* This noisy, beercentric place was built in the late 1990s using surviving elements of the art nouveau architect Victor Horta's Peoples' House in Brussels, scandalously demolished in the 1960s. Culturally enlightening or contrived? Decide for yourself as you tuck into a hearty breakfast or decent brasserie fare with a glass of *gueuze* or an unfiltered Palm.

€€ **Hungry Henrietta**, Lombardenvest 19, **T** 03-232 2928. *Tue-Sat 1200-1400, 1800-2100. Map 2, E5, p252* Enduringly popular with locals, who swear by the 'honest' Belgo-French food (sea bass with asparagus, superior steaks, simply cooked sole). It's a long, narrow restaurant in the heart of the fashion district, with no-frills decor and especially generous portions.

€€ **L'Opera Bouffe**, Arme Duivelstraat 6, **T** 03-226 6413, www.opera-bouffe.be. *Tue-Fri 1200-1500, 1730-2315, Sat 1200-2315. Map 2, F7, p253* This Latin Quarter brasserie is the place to dine if you like nostalgic chanson. Large portions are the order of the day here: all-you-can-eat ribs, lobster, steak and oysters.

€€ **National**, Nationalestraat 32, **T** 03-227 5656, www.ffi.be. *0900-2230, Sun brunch 1000-1400. Map 2, F4, p252* This Italian brasserie, part of the MoMu complex, serves some of the best coffees in town, as well as suitably figure-friendly food: Sicilian fish soup, chicken with sun-dried tomato salad and salmon carpaccio with mozzarella. There's a pretty terrace with an olive tree; inside, it's cool and white, with black tables, a domed ceiling and a giant cactus.

€€ **Zuiderterras**, Ernest van Dijckkaai 37, **T** 03-234 1275, www.zuiderterras.be. *Mon-Thu, Sun 0900-2200, Fri-Sat -2300. Map 2, D2, p252* One of the city's most dramatic settings – Bob Van Reeth's ship-shaped black-and-white building is a waterfront icon, and the white walls and huge mirrors bring the river even closer to your table – and the food doesn't disappoint. Try beef carpaccio with foie gras, scallops with Ganda ham or steamed cod in lemon sabayon.

€ De Bloemkool, Groendalstraat 20, **T** 03-227 3742, www.bloem kool.be. *Mon-Tue, Sun 1130-1730, Wed -1630, Fri-Sat -2130. Map 2, E6, p252* In a modest 17th-century house in the shopping district, this is an ideal venue for lunch, out front on the pavement or in the glass-roofed section at the back. The spaghetti bolognese is great, and the salads are inventive and beautifully presented.

€ Wok A Way, Groendalstraat 14, **T** 03-213 1313, www.wok away.be. *1130-2000. Map 2, E6, p252* Oriental fast food served in a minimalist interior, with high chairs around a communal table.

Cafés

Desiré de Lille, Schrijnwerkersstraat 14-18, **T** 03-232 6226. *Summer 0900-2200, Winter Sun-Thu 0900-2000 and Fri-Sat 0900- 2200. Map 2, E6, p252* Waffle heaven, with a courtyard in which you can scoff on sunny days.

Chez Fred, Kloosterstraat 83, **T** 03-257 1471. *Sun-Wed 0900-2400, Thu-Sat -0300. Map 2, G2, p252* Pause from browsing in antiques shops at this casual, friendly gold-walled café. Enjoy the background jazz music while you dine on generous Italian-style sandwiches, light salads or more refined fish and meat dishes. Popular for breakfast; child-friendly.

Lloyd Loom, Groendalstraat 18, **T** 03-232 6954. *Mon-Sat 0930- 1730. Map 2, E6, p252* The vine-strewn terrace takes a little finding, but it's one of Antwerp's loveliest. Pop in for breakfast, coffee or a light lunch: quiche, salad or home-made lasagne.

Lombardia, Lombardenvest 78, **T** 03-233 6819. *Mon-Sat 0800-1800. Map 2, E5, p252* An organic veggie haunt serving healthy sandwiches, tapas, fresh fruit juices, milkshakes and vegan ice cream.

Pitten and Bonen, Lombardenvest 31, **T** 03-213 2868. *Mon-Sat 0900-1800. Map 2, E5, p252* A colourful café with a peaceful terrace, famed for five-a-day fruit and vegetable cocktails, milkshakes and smoothies (try carrot, parsley and ginger).

Diamond and Jewish districts

Restaurants

€€ Ciro's, Amerikalei 6, **T** 03-238 1147. *Mon-Sat 1100-1400 and 1700-2230, Sun 1100-2230. Map 1, F3, p250* So untrendy that it's now considered 'in', this resolutely old-fashioned establishment serves some of the finest steaks in town.

€€ Hoffy's, Lange Kievitstraat 52, **T** 03-234 3535. *Mon-Thu, Sun 1100-2200, Fri -1600. Map 1, E8, p251* One of Europe's best Yiddish restaurants, founded by the three Hoffman brothers and serving classic kosher dishes. Try chicken with prunes and buckwheat, egg and spinach tart or stuffed aubergines.

€ Beni Falafel, Lange Leemstraat 188, **T** 03-218 8211. *Mon-Sun 1130-1500, 1700-2300, Fri 1130-1600. Map 1, H7, p251* Another institution in the heart of the Jewish district, this time serving excellent vegetarian fast food.

Het Zuid

Restaurants

€€€ Kommilfoo, Vlaamse Kaai 17, **T** 03-237 3000, www.resto.be/kommilfoo. *Wed-Thu 1200-2230, Fri-Sat 1200-2300, Sun 1200-2200. Map 1, F1, p250* There are trendier, friendlier places in the Zuid, but none can hold a candle to the cooking at this prize-winning gastronomic haven. The decor, all cool, neutral browns and greys, and the helpful, unobtrusive staff serve to focus all your attention on the food: king crab with rocket salad, halibut with almond mousseline, red onion soup with Westmalle Triple and, for meat fiends, Camargue bull. Try the *Fantasie van de Chef* menu, determined by the freshest seasonal produce available (four courses €48, or €70 with wine).

€€ **Bar Italia**, Graaf van Egmontstraat 59, **T** 03-216 1748. *Mon-Fri 1200-1430 and 1830-2300, Sat-Sun 1700-2300. Map 1, F2, p250* In typical Antwerp style, this isn't a bar, but a top-notch contemporary Italian restaurant. There are plenty of options for vegetarians, too: oven-cooked veg, pizzas and pasta dishes.

€€ **Bizzie Lizzie**, Vlaamse Kaai 16, **T** 03-238 6197, www.bizzie lizzie.be. *Mon-Fri 1200-1430, 1800-2230, Sat 1800-2300. Map 1, F1, p250* This calm, 'no-nonsense brasserie' with a black and white tiled floor offers a masterclass in low-key chic and unobtrusive service. The cooking is similarly subtle: try sea bass with asparagus and a creamy lemon-orange sauce or Thai-style chicken stew.

€€ **Grand Café Leroy**, Kasteelpleinstraat 49, **T** 03-226 1199. *Mon-Fri 1130-2230, Sat 1830-2330, Sun 1800-2200. Map 1, F3, p250* An upbeat, contemporary-style brasserie offering excellent Belgo-French cuisine and a good-value €16 lunch menu. It's famous for its desserts, including almond tart with smoked bacon caramel sauce. There's a pleasant terrace, too.

€€ **Hippodroom**, Leopold de Waelplaats 10, **T** 03-248 5252, www.hippodroom.be. *Mon-Fri 1200-1430, 1800-2300, no lunch Sat. Map 1, F2, p250* With so many restaurants in this area, attracting repeat custom can be a struggle, but Hippodroom has managed to do just that. The decor is dramatic – crimson banquettes, black tables, huge windows and arty photos – and the food a cut above the (Antwerp) average. Try pike-perch with wild mushroom risotto, bouillabaisse or veal with aubergine caviar. Business lunch €19.

€€ **InVINcible**, Pacificatiestraat 3, **T** 03-294 4878. *1200-1400, 1800-2215. Map 1, G1, p250* Near the new law courts, this stylish place with tall brown leather chairs backs up one of the city's best wine lists with inventive French cuisine: foie gras with sesame and vanilla syrup, duck with caramelized asparagus and balsamic butter sauce, monkfish with artichoke and potato mousseline.

€€ **Lucy Chang**, Marnixplaats 17, **T** 03-248 9560, www.lucy chang.be. *Daily 1200-2400. Map 1, F2, p250* Delicate, fragrant oriental dishes in a wooden, eastern minimal interior. On the menu: Vietnamese, Thai and Cantonese soups, satay, spring rolls, excellent dim sum and Thai and Malaysian curries.

€€ **O'Tagine**, Leopold de Waelstraat 20, **T** 03-237 0619. *1200-1500, 1730-2300, Sat-Sun -2400. Map 1, G1, p250* Despite the name, there's not a hint of Oirishness in this Moroccan restaurant. The decor is Moorish, the background sounds are authentic and the tagines are excellent: try chicken with lemon and olives or almonds and raisins. Moroccan wines, too.

€€ **Soeki**, Volkstraat 21, **T** 03-238 7505. *Tue-Thu and Sun 1800-2300, Fri-Sat 1800-2400. Map 1, F2, p250* Young bohemians flock to this harem-style affair to sit on cushions around low tables and wash down tapas with cocktails, wine, world music and indie rock.

€€ **Zuid**, Volkstraat 69, **T** 03-248 8189. *Mon-Fri from 0800, Sat-Sun from 1000. Map 1, F2, p250* A great people-watching perch, with a glass veranda and views down to the Fine Arts Museum. Fusion food is the thing here: wok-cooked vegetables with coconut milk and Thai spices, Ardennes trout with saffron or wild sea bass in a polenta crust with tomato salsa. There's a good choice of wines, and the mint tea is marvellous.

€ De Broers van Julienne, Kasteelpleinstraat 45, **T** 03-232 0203, www.debroersvanjulienne.be. *Mon-Sat 1200-2200, Sun 1730-2200. Map 1, F3, p250* Inventive meat-free restaurant with a delightful terrace. There's a good choice of quiches and soups, or try Moroccan carrot salad, cheese tempura, aubergine lasagne or fish tagine.

€ Funky Soul Potato, Volkstraat 76, **T** 03-257 0744. *1200-2400. Map 1, F2, p250* Cheap, cheerful and just a little cramped, this noisy eatery serves baked potatoes – tuna, merguez and ratatouille, ham and cheese – with mounds of salad. Great for children.

Cafés

De Nieuwe Linde, Pacificatiestraat 49, **T** 03-248 1486. *Daily from 1700. Map 1, G1, p250* Until the late 1990s, this was *the* literary café in Antwerp. Fashion may have deserted it, but charm certainly hasn't: it's a great place to sit and read a book with one eye on the local characters.

L'Entrepot du Congo, Vlaamse Kaai 42, **T** 03-257 1648. *Daily 0800-late. Map 1, F1, p250* One of the oldest bistro-bars on the quays, the ironically named Congo Warehouse continues to attract an alternative crowd. The interior is quintessential shabby chic, with a black and white tiled floor and mirrored wood panels.

Zurich, Verlatstraat 2, **T** 03-238 4867. *Mon-Fri from 0730, Sat-Sun from 1000. Map 1, F1, p250* Another deliberately downmarket bar-café-restaurant, with echoes of L'Entrepot du Congo. The decor's lighter and brighter, though, and the huge slanted mirror on one wall is a nice touch.

't Eilandje

Restaurants

€€ **Bassin**, Tavernierkaai, **T** 03-225 3637, www.bassin.be. *Daily 1000-2300, Sat 1800-late, Sun 1200-2200. Map 1, A3, p250* At this cheerful brasserie with a riverside terrace, traditional Flemish cooking is prepared 'grandma's way'. It serves the city's best *stoofvlees* (beef stewed in beer) and *stoemp*; bolder hearts might fancy ox tongue with Madeira and mushrooms. Chips are served with the appropriate pomp, in fancy copper stands.

€€ **Het Pomphuis**, Siberiasstraat, **T** 03-770 8625, www.het pomphuis.be. *1200-1430 and 1800-2230. Map 1, A11, p251* Once a pump house, now a huge, high-ceilinged brasserie with arched windows and burgundy walls. Bag a table with a dockside view and feast on scallops with spinach and mustard, prawns with penne and olives or lamb fillet with pesto and peas. Business lunch €23.

€€ **La Riva**, Londenstraat 52, **T** 03-225 0102, www.lariva.be. *Sun-Fri 1200-1500, 1800, Sat 1800-late. Map 1, C12, p251* Another stunning conversion, this time a beautifully converted dockers' shelter. On summer evenings, sunlight streams in, giving this vast, dark-brown, high-ceilinged venue a delightful glow. The food gives the place a run for its money: tomato gazpacho with crab *loempia*, duck fillet with black truffles and bream with aubergine compote and basil mayonnaise. Watch out for the weekend DJs.

€€ **Lux**, Adriaan Brouwerstraat 13, **T** 03-233 3030, www.lux antwerp.com. *1200-1430 and 1800-2300, no lunch Sat. Map 1, A3, p250* Yet another stunning conversion, in an 18th-century house, with plush wood panelling, a monumental staircase and a cool, contemporary grey and black colour scheme. The food is brilliant

Belgo-Med – gazpacho, prawn croquettes, smoked duck and chorizo salad with raspberries, super-duper steaks – and thoughtful touches abound. Even a carafe of house wine comes with a smart tag telling you all about the vintage. Lunch €20.

Cafés

€ **De Eetkamer**, Napoleonkaai 43, **T** 03-227 1648, www.de-eetkamer.be. *Tue-Fri 0800-1900.* *Map 1, C11, p251* A popular, beautifully situated lunch and breakfast venue on the Willemdok marina, serving straightforward salads and top-notch pasta.

Zurenborg

Restaurants

€€€ **Dôme sur Mer**, Arendstraat 1, **T** 03-239 9093, www.dome web.be. *Tue-Sun 1700-0100.* *Map 1, G8, p251* Is it a kitchen design shop? An aquarium? No, it's Antwerp's hottest seafood venue, an ultramodern, white-walled affair with a long fish tank along the wall and fresh oysters, fish soup and scallops on the menu.

€€ **Brasserie van Loock**, Dageraadplaats 10-11, **T** 03-235 0158, *Mon-Fri 1200-1430, 1800-2230, Sat 1800-2300.* *Map 1, G9, p251* Big, bustling bar-brasserie on one of the city's most appealing squares. The decor is very Antwerp, with beautiful lights, dark walls and high ceilings, but the food is reassuringly Belgian: steaks, shrimp croquettes, beer-stewed beef and chips, chips, chips.

€€ **Comcarmenne**, Dageraadplaats 19, **T** 03-236 1506. *Mon, Wed-Fri 1200-1400 and 1800-2200, Sat-Sun 1800-2200.* *Map 1, G9, p251* A bright, family-friendly eatery that pulls off the neo-retro look – brown tables, red cushions and roses – without feeling studied or sterile. The eclectic menu spans curries, vegetarian lasagne and tapas.

€€ **El Warda**, Draakstraat 4, **T** 03-239 3113. *Tue-Sun 1800-2400. Map 1, G9, p251* A sensationally good North African restaurant. The Tunisian chef, Fatima Marzouki, has written several cookbooks, and her couscous and tagines are fabulously delicate and tasty. Booking essential.

€€ **Euterpia**, Generaal Capiaumontstraat 2, **T** 03-235 0202. *Wed-Sun from 1900-late. Map 1, H10, p251* Housed in a striking art nouveau building with a garden and covered terrace, this restaurant is frequented by an arty crowd: Keith Haring did the label for the house wine. The cuisine proves the French and Belgians really can get along: cod steamed with capers or *coucou de Malines* (Belgium's answer to *poulet de Bresse*) in puff pastry with a wild mushroom and truffle sauce.

Cafés

Wattman, Tramplein 3, **T** 03-230 5540, www.wattman.be. *Tue-Fri from 1000, Sat-Sun from 0900. Map 1, G9, p251* Right at the top of Cogels-Osylei, this is a charming, slightly ramshackle bohemian haunt, with good, simple cooking, and shelves bursting with toys for children.

Borgerhout

€€ **Ecocafé**, Turnhoutsebaan 139, **T** 03-663 3656. *Tue-Sat 1000-2200, Sun -2000. Map 1, D10, p251* The café at the Ecohuis is a safe bet for starving vegetarians, though on this evidence, the Belgian vision of a greener, cleaner world finds space for socking great steaks.

Ghent

Restaurants

€€€ Allegro Moderato, Korenlei 7, **T** 09-233 2332, www.resto
allegro.com. *Tue-Sat 1145-1500 and 1800-2200. Map 3, E2, p254*
Romantic, candlelit riverside restaurant with timeless decor,
classical background music and Franco-Med cuisine: baby lobster
with asparagus and truffle oil, red mullet with ratatouille and lamb
with mustard and tarragon.

€€€ Belga Queen, Graslei 10, **T** 09-280 0100, www.belga
queen.be. *Daily 1200-1430, 1900-2400. Map 3, F2, p254* A recent
addition to Antonio Pinto's restaurant empire, this lopsided
Romanesque granary has a medieval-meets-industrial feel, with
leather armchairs and glorious river views. The menu takes Belgian
cuisine to new extremes, offering only locally farmed produce and
wines from Belgian-run vineyards across the world: try eels in
Chimay beer, ham knuckle with *peket* (Liège gin), snails with
gueuze butter or duck liver with Belgian vermouth.

€€€ Jan Breydel, Jan Breydelstraat 10, **T** 09-225 6287. *1200-
1330, 1900-2130. Map 3, D2, p254* Romantic riverside restaurant
with one of the loveliest terraces in town. Excellent fish and
seafood dishes, including an exquisite lobster bisque, and local
classics such as *waterzooï*.

€€ Coeur d'Artichaut, Onderbergen 6, **T** 09-225 3318,
www.artichaut.be. *Tue-Sat 1200-1430, 1900-2230. Map 3, H1, p255*
This stylish modern brasserie, housed in a high-ceilinged 19th-
century mansion, has a lovely walled patio out back. The cooking is
suitably sunny: scallop salad with pine nuts, guinea fowl with wild
rice and caramelized endive, monkfish in red wine sauce with risotto.

Eating

€€ De Foyer, Sint-Baafsplein 17, **T** 09-225 3275, www.theater cafedefoyer.be. *1200-late. Map 3, G5, p255* The views of the Belfry and St Bavo's Cathedral from the first-floor terrace are reason enough to eat at the KNS theatre's brasserie, so the quality of the cooking is a bonus. Steak, sole and mussels are present and correct, but if you've overdone it on the Belgian staples, goat's cheese salad with a raspberry coulis should hit the spot. Lunch menu €12.50.

€€ De Hel, Kraanlei 81, **T** 09-224 3240. *Wed-Sun, 1800-2200. Map 3, C4, p254* Plush, cosy and extremely hospitable restaurant with a remarkable red-brick rococo façade. It comes into its own in winter, with hearty stews, *waterzooï* and rabbit dishes.

€€ Domestica, Onderbergen 27, **T** 09-223 5300. *Sat-Fri 1200-1500 and 1830-2300, Mon 1830-2300. Map 3, H2, p255* A brand-new brasserie and bar offering good French food in a spectacular setting, with wooden floors, chocolate walls and handsome chandeliers. The garden is delightful, and there's a roaring fire in winter.

€€ Graaf van Egmond, Sint-Michielsplein 21, **T** 09-225 0727, *1200-1400, 1800-2200. Map 3, G1, p255* Tempting as the terrace is, you need to make for the romantic first-floor room to enjoy fine views of the Graslei and down-the-line Flemish food: eels in herb sauce, creamy chicken *waterzooï*, steak and shrimp croquettes.

€€ Grade, De Kerckhovelaan 79, **T** 09-224 4385, www.grade.be. *1200-1400, 1830-2230. Map 3, off L3 (off map), p255* A must if you're visiting SMAK or the Fine Arts Museum, this trendy lounge/restaurant with smart black and orange decor has one of the best kitchens in town. The mod Med dishes include salmon with aubergine tapenade, linguine with grey shrimps and a creamy herb sauce and astoundingly tender tuna with capers and olives.

Eating

€€ **HA'**, Kouter 29, **T** 09-265 9181. *Tue-Sat 1100-2300, Sun 0900-1600.* Map 3, J5, p255 Popular, high-ceilinged brasserie in the former stock exchange, now a concert venue with a restaurant and canalside bar. Dine on chicken fillet with ratatouille, cod with mustard and broccoli puree or steak with pepper sauce at sleek brown tables between sunny yellow walls.

€€ **The House of Eliott**, Jan Breydelstraat 36, **T** 09-225 2128, www.thehouseofeliott.be. *Thu-Mon, 1200-1400, 1800-late.* Map 3, D2, p254 Yes, as in Louise Lombard and Stella Gonet: the convivial owners are both fans of the TV series, and the 1920s-style decor of their lovely canalside restaurant pays it theatrical tribute. There's a fusion theme to the food: try artichoke with Serrano ham and pine nuts, veal with coffee sauce, monkfish with asparagus and chorizo or one of the luscious lobster dishes.

€€ **Mineral**, Onderbergen 25, **T** 09-224 0458, www.mineral.be. *Mon-Sat 1200-1400, 1800-2400.* Map 3, H1, p255 Good-value Franco-Mediterranean cuisine – Sicilian-style sardines, salade niçoise, tuna with home-made tagliatelle, spag bol with pancetta and Provençal herbs – in a setting that blends rustic, formal and ultra-modern to spectacular effect. Popular at lunchtime, when there's a €20 menu (or €15 for vegetarians) and a dish of the day.

€€ **Pakhuis**, Schuurkenstraat 4, **T** 09-223 5555, www.pakhuis.be. *Mon-Sat, restaurant 1200-1430 and 1830 to 2400, bar 1130-0100.* Map 3, G3, p255 Another Antonio Pinto conversion, this time a vast space with a military-green colour scheme, classical pillars and statues, impossibly high ceilings and scores of fans whose whirring brings *Apocalypse Now* to mind. There's a brasserie buzz, but the Italo-French cuisine has real flair – salad with shrimps and artichoke, ham in Tierenteyn mustard, sea bass carpaccio. The bar snacks are among the best in town.

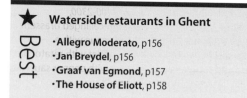

★ **Waterside restaurants in Ghent**

Best

- **Allegro Moderato**, p156
- **Jan Breydel**, p156
- **Graaf van Egmond**, p157
- **The House of Eliott**, p158

€€ **Raj**, Kraanlei 43, **T** 09-234 3459, www.raj.be. *Wed-Mon from 1800, Sat-Sun 1200-late. Map 3, C3, p254* From the deliciously authentic decor to the excellent teas, this knocks your average curry house for six: sink into a cushion, or sit in the lovely courtyard, and you could almost be in Rajasthan. Sample the excellent cooking by having the *rijsttafel* (€18), which gets you two meat or vegetarian curries with rice. The complex also houses a bathhouse and a gallery of Indian artefacts.

€€ **'T Klokhuys**, Corduwaniersstraat 65, **T** 09-223 4241. *1200-1415, 1800-2300. Map 3, C3, p254* It's somewhat disorientating to be surrounded by clocks that all tell different times; that aside, this child-friendly brasserie offers reasonably priced Flemish favourites: *waterzooï*, beer-stewed beef, and ham with Tierenteyn mustard.

€€ **Vier Tafels**, Plotersgracht 6, **T** 09-226 0525. *1200-1400, 1800-2230, no lunch Mon. Map 3, C3, p254* Around the world in 80 plates? That's the mission statement at this lively, foliage-filled restaurant, which offers a whistle-stop tour of global specialities, from Bulgarian iced cucumber soup to kangaroo steak via Cantonese-style rattlesnake.

€ **Avalon**, Geldmunt 32, **T** 09-224 3724. *1200-1400. Map 3, C2, p254* Tasty, good-value organic vegetarian eatery, offering quiches, pasta, salads and stews in a bright, fresh decor.

Eating

€ Souplounge, Zuivelbrugstraat 6, **T** 09-223 6203, www.souplounge.be. *Tue-Sun 1000-1900. Map 3, C4, p254* The bright 1970s-style decor is a cheery setting in which to snack on good fresh soups and generous salads.

Cafés

Brooderie, Jan Breydelstraat 8, **T** 09-225 0623. *0800-1800, Tue 1130-1700. Map 3, E2, p254* Next to the lovely Appelbrug park, this modest eatery with a wooden interior serves healthy breakfasts and vegetarian snacks, including delicious quiches.

Friet Lounge, Normaalschoolstraat 47, **T** 0494-633740, www.frietlounge.com. *Mon-Fri 1130-1430, 1700-late. Map 3, off L3 (off map), p255* It's a chip shop, but not as we know it: lounge about to soothing chillout tunes after a night of partying, and feast on the freshest of frites with homemade mayonnaise.

Greenway Goods, Nederkouter 42, **T** 09-269 0769. *1100-2100. Map 3, L3, p255* An organic snack bar, famous for its veggie burgers and cleansing vegetable juices.

Mosquito Coast, Serpentstraat 5, **T** 09-224 3720. *Tue-Sun from 1500. Map 3, D5, p254* A 'travel and adventure' café where you can plot your next holiday while nibbling tapas or sampling some ethnic cuisine.

Pain Perdu, Walpoortstraat 9, **T** 09-224 1825. *Mon-Sat 1130-0100. Map 3, L6, p254* A laid-back, high-ceilinged café, with a grandiose faux-baroque interior and a pretty garden. A great spot for brunch.

Eating

Finding a great bar in Antwerp or Ghent is like falling off a log – and if you don't respect the potency of the local brews, you risk doing precisely that. Antwerp claims to have more than 4000 drinking dens (roughly 1 per 100 residents), a greater concentration than in any other city; at the last count, Ghent had 288 in its centre alone. In both cities, bars stay open late, even on weekdays; most places are open after midnight, and if the place you're in closes, you'll face a gruelling walk of 50 or maybe even 100 m to find somewhere to get in the next few rounds. Most offer at least 20 draught and bottled brews, while the specialist beer bars have menus running into the hundreds.

The clubbing scene is limited by comparison, but both cities have world-renowned nightspots and a more alternative scene. For Antwerp listings, check out *Zone 03*, the free weekly newspaper, and the *Week Up* calendar (www.weekup.be), both widely available; in Ghent, look out for *Zone 09*. For more information about parties, visit www.antwerpisburning.be, www.noctis.com, www.nightclubbing.be and www.5voor12.com.

Historic centre

Bars

Buster, Kaasrui 1, **T** 03-232 5153, www.busterpodium.be. *Tue-Sat, 2000-late. Map 2, C3, p252* Cosy venue for (mostly free) jazz and folk concerts, with an emphasis on up-and-coming talents.

Café au Lait, Oude Beurs 8, **T** 03-225 1981. *Mon-Fri 1800-late, Sat-Sun 2000-late. Map 2, B4, p252* Fans of funky beats flock to this small, smoky bar off the Grote Markt to get down to a soundtrack of Afrobeat, R&B, soul and reggae. The bright red-and-orange walls are jazzed up with tribal masks.

De Muze, Melkmarkt 15, **T** 03-226 0126. *1100-0300. Map 2, D5, p252* Another Antwerp institution, this jazz bar was at the centre of the city's 1960s counterculture and still has a smoky boho feel. Three cavernous storeys of exposed brick and wood, it's vast enough to absorb the tourists and leave room for local Kerouac wannabes. Good live bands; entertainingly bolshie bar staff.

Den Engel, Grote Markt 3, **T** 03-233 1252. *0900-late. Map 2, C4, p252* An Antwerp institution, 'The Angel' buzzes with the chatter of excited locals. With good views of the cathedral from the terrace, it's a handy spot for listening to a summer carillon concert.

Den Heksenketel, Pelgrimstraat 22, **T** 03-226 1928. *Mon-Fri 1600-late, Sat-Sun 1400-late. Map 2, D4, p252* This sociable café specializes in live folk music – but with not a hint of earnest beardiness. Dress to sweat, not in a sweater, as dancing is de rigueur.

De Pelikaan, Melkmarkt 14, **T** 03-227 2351. *Wed-Mon, 1000-late. Map 2, D5, p252* No snacks, just booze: it's a simple formula, but one that's worked for 50 years. The decor, music and, crucially, the prices have hardly changed down the decades. Regulars play cards into the small hours or until they can no longer see straight.

De Vagant, Reyndersstraat 25, **T** 03-233 1538. *Mon-Fri 1100-late, Sat-Sun 1200-late. Map 2, D4, p252* If you want to try the local firewater, look no further than this cosy bar off Groenplaats. There's a vast range of young, old and flavoured *jenevers* (juniper gin), which you can chase with a *bolleke* if you so desire.

La Bodeguita, Ernst van Dijckkaai 21, **T** 03-226 0112. *Thu-Sun, 2000-late. Map 2, D2, p252* The city's most famous salsa spot, though its repertoire stretches to merengue, rumba and bachato. Especially lively around midnight on weekends; regulars go on Thursdays.

Raga, Hendrik Conscienceplein 11, **T** 03-485 6656. *Mon-Sat, 1200- late. Map 2, C6, p252* A small, smart and civilized wine bar in the shadow of Carolus Borromeus church with a well-chosen wine list.

't Elfde Gebod, Torfbrug 10, **T** 03-289 3466. *1000-late. Map 2, C5, p252* Hard by the cathedral, the 'Eleventh Commandment' is a riot of tacky religious artefacts. Kitschiness, it seems, is next to godliness: there's an almost church-like hush, as clients contemplate the otherworldly qualities of a draught Westmalle Dubbel to a backdrop of classical music.

't Waagstuk, Stadswaag 20, **T** 03-225 0219. *Mon-Fri 1000-0200, Sat 1400-0400, Sun 1400-0200. Map 2, A7, p253* The Stadswaag square comes alive at night, but this brown café, with its pretty courtyard and one of the best beer lists in town, suits daytime drinking.

Witzli-Poetzli, Blauwmoezelstraat 4, **T** 03-232 9120. *1000-late. Map 2, C5, p252* The haunt of would-be poets and intellectuals,

> ### Mine's a pintje!

If you don't want to order a beer in English, and aren't sure how to pronounce the names on the menu, here are a few fail-safe options.

For a 25cl lager (Stella, Jupiler, Maes et al): "een pintje" (pronounced "*ain pint-tchye*").

For a De Koninck: "een bolleke" – if you can't manage to keep a straight face, you can also ask for "een prinske", but the glass is frankly effeminate.

For instant barfly credibility: "een Duveltje" ("*ain Doovel-tchye*") – means 'a little Duvel', as if knocking back 8.5% beers is the sort of thing you do for breakfast.

For aficionado status: "een Trappist" – will procure a rich, dark Westmalle Dubbel from the tap.

And the best way to order a Hoegaarden? Try "A white beer, please".

who gather in the morning to discuss what they intend to write – but end up drinking all day. It's not as pretentious as it sounds, just plain hedonistic, and the music ranges from chanson to tango.

Clubs

Café SOS, Zakstraat 4, www.shotonstage.org. *Tue-Sun, 1900-late. Map 2, B4, p252* A small venue with a seriously eclectic music policy: from ska, dub and reggae to avant-electronica and 'bliptriphiphop' evenings.

De Cinema, Lange Brilstraat 12, **T** 03-234 0257, www.decinema.be. *Wed-Sun, 2200 or 2300-late. Map 2, A7, p253* The neoclassical façade of this former cinema scarcely prepares you for the futuristic-industrial decor. Ciné Soirée is a student party run by the hip Flemish radio station Studio Brussel (Thu) and Couleur d'Anvers (Sat) serving up dancefloor-friendly hip-hop, soul and R&B.

Sint-Andries and the Latin Quarter

Bars

Bar 2, Vrijdagmarkt 19, **T** 03-227 5436. *Wed, Thu, Sat 1000-late, Fri 0800-late, Sun 1200-2000. Map 2, E4, p252* On a square that's not short of bars and cafés, 'Bar Deux' attracts a trendy crowd and has great views of the elegant Plantin-Moretus Museum from its terrace. Good foccacias and friendly, if overworked, staff.

Café Kulminator, Vleminckveld 32-34, **T** 03-232 4538. *Mon 2000-2400, Tue-Fri 1200-2400, Sat 1700-2400, closed Sun. Map 2, F5, p252* If you're after style, move swiftly on; if beer is the key, you'll probably never leave. There are more than 500 varieties on offer – some say 900 – including several that have been maturing for decades.

Dansing Chocola, Kloosterstraat 161, **T** 0486 600459. *0800-0100. Map 2, H2, p252* Just the kind of place you want to tumble into after an afternoon's antiques-browsing: arty, laid-back and hospitable, with knowingly ramshackle decor. Be warned, though: tables and chairs in the pretty upstairs gallery are a little precarious.

De Duifkens, Graanmarkt 5, **T** 03-225 1039. *Mon-Fri from 1100, Sat from 1000, Sun 1000-2000. Map 2, F7, p253* A tiny, blissfully old-fashioned and smoky local in the Latin Quarter, plastered with photographs of actors and famous for its huge sandwiches.

Clubs

Den Aalmoezenier, Aaalmoezenierstraat 4, **T** 03-225 0585, www.denaalmoezenier.be. *Thu-Sat, 2200-late. Map 2, G4, p252* This small, grungy backstreet venue is by far your best bet for an indie night. Sat night is '*Het Alternatief*'.

Genever convention
To blend in with the locals, chase a flavoured Flemish gin with a bolleke *of Antwerp-brewed De Koninck beer.*

Ile Afrik, Aalmoezenierstraat 13, **T** 03-231 1741, www.ileafrik.com.
Tue, Thu 2000-late, Fri-Sat 2200-late. Map 2, G4, p252 R&B, African,
Latin and Afro-Caribbean music. The walls are hung with African
and, less predictably, Batman masks.

Diamond and Jewish districts

Clubs

Café Capital, Rubenslei 37, www.cafecapital.be. *Fri and Sat 2300-late Map ,1, E5, p250* Though the buildings resemble a slightly grim park cafeteria, this is not a café at all, but one of the city's coolest clubs, with dEUS star Tom Barman and Berlin's *Phonique* among those who've manned the decks.

't Eilandje

Bars

Bar du Port, Napoleonkaai 53. *Sat-Wed 0900-2400, Thu-Fri 0900-0300. Map 1, C12, p251* Friendly and popular quayside bar with an old-fashioned wood-panelled interior.

Cappuccino Club, St Laureiskaai 13, www.cappuccinoclub.be. *Tue-Sat, 1400-late. Map 1, C11, p251* A fun place with a cultivated down-at-heel look where people go for a drink, but usually end up dancing, to beats that are anything but repetitive.

Fake Bar, Kattendijkdok. *Thu-Sun, seemingly at all hours. Map 1, A11, p251* In the same grain silo as Extra City (see p89), this may just be the city's finest bar: great music, a cool (not cliquey) crowd and a delicious sense of abandon. Outside, there's a 'beach' with deckchairs and dockside views, perfect for a Sunday barbecue.

Kaaiman, Napelsstraat 57, **T** 0486-477033, www.kaaiman.be. *Wed-Sun, 2000. Map 1, C12, p251* Hard to find, and even harder to pin down, this venue is almost too eclectic for its own good: a lounge bar with local DJs on Wednesday and Sunday, a venue for rock, avant-jazz and electronica concerts on Thursday and a club on Friday and Saturday, when the music ranges from twisted techno to Afro-funk.

Licht der Dokken, Verbindingsdok-Westkaai 2, **T** 0475 490878. *From 1000. Map 1, C11, p251* A minuscule corner bar with mirrored panels, glass cabinets, lace in the windows and an old wooden drink-up bell – a classic local basically, but one that the city's tastemakers have decreed the apogee of cool. Which is handy, as you can venture in without attracting stares.

Clubs

Café d'Anvers, Verversrui 15, **T** 03-226 3870, www.cafedanvers. com. *Fri, Sat, 2200-late. Map 1, A3, p250* Once a church, now the city's foremost temple of techno, attracting clubbers from Holland and Paris. Deep house and techno grooves for an up-for-it crowd, with guest spots by the likes of Laurent Garnier and Bob Sinclar.

Roxy/Red&Blue/Studio 54, Lange Schipperskapelstraat 11-13, **T** 03-213 0555, www.redandblue.be, www.studio54antwerp.be. *Fri, Sat 2300-late, Sun 2200-late. Map 1, A3, p250* These are the regular nights at this multi-purpose venue. Roxy is happy house with an Ibiza vibe; Red&Blue, on Saturday, is one of Europe's best gay nights (men only); Studio 54 is all about disco decadence.

! In summer, the Rijnkaai acquires a beach-hut bar and outside deckchairs. Come here to enjoy the evening play of light on the Scheldt and ponder the fate of those who took the Red Star Line.

Het Zuid

Bars

Bar Tabac, Waalse Kaai 43, **T** 03-238 1937. *1900-late, winter Tue-Sun, 2000-late. Map 1, off F1, p250* The original and genuine. This was one of the first bars in the Zuid, and it's still one of the coolest. The rough, 1950s truck-stop look gives it an edge some of its smoother neighbours can't match and it's open ridiculously late.

Boogaloo, Jan van Beersstraat 1, **T** 03-232 5153, www.boogaloo. be. *Tue-Sun 1600-late. Map 1, H1, p250* Unpretentious dance café, with an eclectic music mix and good cocktails.

De Scene, Graaf van Hoornestraat 2, **T** 03-238 6462. *1700-late. Map 1, G1, p250* An alternative hangout that's as rough-hewn and rocky as the Zuid gets. Fans of surf rock and grunge will love it.

The Heming Way, Waalse Kaai 19, **T** 03-248 4769. *Tue-Sat, 2000-late, Fri 1600-late. Map 1, F1, p250* Kick off your night with an aperitif at this smart establishment. Ernest would doubtless have approved of the atmosphere, if not the spelling.

Hopper, Leopold de Waelstraat 2, **T** 03-248 4933. *1030-late. Map 1, F1, p250* The night owls at this long-established jazz café tend to be older and more intellectual than those at its rowdier counterparts. Check out the live concerts (Sun 1600, Mon 2130).

Mogador, Graaf van Egmontstraat 57, **T** 03-238 7160, www.moga dor.be. *1700-late. Map 1, F2, p250* Those who count themselves among the beautiful people will enjoy this slightly intimidating lounge bar. Pre-club DJ sets and an upmarket wine and cocktail list.

Patine, Leopold de Waelstraat 1, **T** 03-257 0919. *Mon-Thu 0800-0100, Fri-Sun 0900-0200. Map 1, F1, p250* Delightful and relaxed wine bar. The wine list is long and eminently affordable; if you overdo it, there's a B&B upstairs (see p130).

Sips, Gillisplaats 8, **T** 03-257 3959. *1700 or 1800-late. Map 1, F1, p250* Cocktails and cigars are the specialities here (the bartender used to work on the QE2). The range of spirits is among the city's finest and two terraces beckon for that Hamlet moment.

Clubs

Petrol, d'Herbouvillekaai 21, **T** 03-226 4963, www.petrolclub.be. *Usually Fri, Sat, 2300-late. Map 1, off F1 (off map), p250* It's a fair trek along the waterfront, but well worth it for the city's coolest club-cum-concert venue. The line-ups are eclectic – A Certain Ratio, Luke Slater, Roni Size, The Kills and Muggs from Cypress Hill – and atmosphere, not attitude, is the key to its popularity.

Velvet Lounge, Luikstraat 6, **T** 03-237 3978, www.velvetlounge.be. *1130-1700 and 1800-late. Map 1, F1, p250* A 21st-century take on the dinner dance: a fusion restaurant in a retro-colonial setting, bathed in orange light, with chillout, lounge and jazz tunes spun by the in-house DJ. In the same complex, **Stereo Sushi**, **T** 03-248 6727, www.stereo sushi.be, offers slick sounds, sushi and 1950s manga decor.

Zurenborg

Bars

Zeezicht, Dageraadplaats 7-8, **T** 03-235 1065. *1200-late. Map 1, G9, p251* Tucked into a corner of the neighbourhood's most sociable square, and with its biggest terrace, this place has a reputation for being left-wing. The talk here is more cultural than political, though, and the arty young crowd gets fairly animated as the evening wears on. There's a festival here in late May.

Borgerhout

Bars

De Kroon, Kerkstraat 91, **T** 03-235 1123. *From 0800, closed Tue. Map 1, C9, p251* This former billiards café is trendy in a typically downhome Antwerp way: popular with artists and a supercool selection of jazz and rock on the stereo. There's no table service.

Plaza Real, Kattenberg 93, **T** 03-235 5212. *Tue-Sun 1100-late. Map 1, D10, p251* Run by the violinist from dEUS and his partner, Plaza Real is a small but perfectly formed alternative outpost in an otherwise unfashionable neighbourhood. Convivial and cutting-edge with flea-market furniture and relentlessly fabulous music.

Ghent

Pick up USE-IT'S indispensable *Cafeplan* for an irreverent precis of all the city's cafés and bars, as well as a map. We've been out with these guys, and they know how to have a good time. If you want to hang out with the local students, head for Overpoortstraat, south of the city centre, home to scores of bars. Metalheads should check out the seriously hardcore gigs at **Frontline** (Nos 35-37); jungle bunnies should check out **Decadance** at No 76 (www.decadance.be).

Bars

Charlatan, Vlasmarkt 6, **T** 09-224 2457, www.charlatan.be. *Tue-Sun 1900-late. Map 3, D7, p254* At the epicentre of one of the city's nightlife hubs, this is a genuinely alternative bar and concert venue, with frequent live gigs and wildly eclectic sounds.

De Dulle Griet, Vrijdagmarkt 50, **T** 09-224 2455. *Daily 1200-0100. Map 3, D4, p254* Crammed with puppets and other bric-a-brac, Mad Meg is a classic brown café with hundreds of beers on offer. The house speciality is Kwak Max – a huge glass containing more than two pints of strong beer. They make for great souvenirs, which is why you have to hand over a shoe when you order one.

Dreupelkot, Groentenmarkt 12, **T** 09-224 2120. *1600-late. Map 3, E3, p254* Genever is the speciality here, with 215 kinds on offer and generous measures. Drink standing up to bolster your cred.

Folklore, Lange Steenstraat 69, **T** 09-224 3118. *Sun-Thu 0800-2000; Fri 0800-0100; Sat 1100-2400. Map 3, A3, p254* One of the city's last authentic brown bars, this is a place where a moustache can be worn without irony. The decor has a decidedly 1970s feel, and some of the regulars may not have left since then. The tunes come from the old-fashioned jukebox and you can try your hand at an incomprehensible Belgian bar game or tuck into a fresh raw-meat sandwich (Fridays only).

Gainsbar, Oudburg 51, **T** 09-225 1969. *Tue-Sun 2000-late. Map 3, B4, p254* A humorous homage to chanson – urbane, rather than kitsch – decorated with singles by, and photos of, Johnny Hallyday, Jacques Brel, Piaf, Cloclo and their ilk. One wall is plastered with faded magazine covers; check out *Brigitte Bardot's Comic Strip*.

Hotsy Totsy, Hoogstraat 1, **T** 09-224 2012, www.hotsytotsy.be. *Tue-Sun 2000-late. Map 3, off F1 (off map), p254* This step-gabled medieval house is now home to a bustling jazz café. Inside, there's a deco feel, with stained glass, tasselled lampshades, sepia photos of jazz musicians and a palpable Prohibition atmosphere.

On yer bike

With nearly 300 bars in the city centre alone, you won't have to go far to find a Ghent watering hole to suit your tastes.

Jos, Vlasmarkt 7. *Wed-Sat 1500-0200. Map 3, D7, p254* An offshoot of the Charlatan, for people who were going to gigs before the Charlatan's clientele had even been born. The tunes are similar, but the vibe is more laid-back and refined.

Limonada, Heilige Geeststraat 7, **T** 09-233 7885, www.limonada. be. *Mon-Sat, 1930-late. Map 3, G4, p255* A stylish lounge bar with 1970s decor and luminous furniture to match.

Pink Flamingo's, Onderstraat 55, **T** 09-233 4718. *Daily 1200, Thu and Fri 'til 0300, Sat 1400-0300, Sun 1400-0000. Map 3, D5, p254* This knowingly kitsch hangout is stuffed with secular and religious icons, ranging from Christ to Princess Di. The relaxed atmosphere and leftfield music draw a mixed, chatty crowd.

Rococo, Corduwaniersstraat 57. *Tue-Sun from 2100. Map 3, C3, p254* In the mood for romance? It's hard to beat this high-ceilinged beauty, with gorgeous stuccowork, guttering candles and classical music warbling gently in the backround. Try the 'love elixir', a sweet aperitif made to a secret recipe, or take a seat at the piano. There are logs in one corner, ready for a roaring fire in winter.

't Velootje, Kalversteeg 2, **T** 09-223 2834. *Tue-Sat from 1800. Map 3, B4, p254* The 'Little Bike' is cluttered with junk and vintage bicycles, amassed by the Catweazle-esque owner. In a prime Patershol location, it's touristy (and slightly overpriced) but fun.

Vintage, Onderbergen 35, **T** 09-223 5132. *1130-1400, 1800-0100. Map 3, I2, p255* Laid-back wine bar with an excellent global list and hearty Med or Belgian cold plates. French-speaking wine buffs can play the Trivial Pursuit 'Edition des Vins' as they quaff.

Vooruit, Sint-Pietersnieuwstraat 23, **T** 09-267 2848, www.vooruit. be. *1130-0200, Fri-Sat until 0300. Map 3, off L6 (off map), p255*
Vast, airy café in the Vooruit Arts Centre. Cheap food and DJs on Saturday nights, entertaining a predictably trendy young crowd, . Check www.kozzmozz.com for hip-hop, techno or drum'n'bass nights in the centre itself.

Waterhuis aan de Bierkant, Groentenmarkt 9, **T** 09-225 0680. *1100-late. Map 3, E3, p254* Offers upwards of 100 beers (on a menu with wince-worthy puns in four languages) and one of the best terraces in town. You'll face stiff competition for a canalside seat.

Clubs

Culture Club, Afrikalaan 147, **T** 09-267 6440, www.cultureclub.be. *Fri and Sat 2300-late, check website for dates/tickets. Map 3, off A8 (off map), p254* For party people, this is Ghent's biggest attraction. *Sunday Times Style* dubbed it "the coolest club in the world" and it's listed in Wikipedia's all-time top 30, along with giants such as Studio 54. The secret? As anyone who's heard 2 Many DJs will know, it's being unpretentious, unpredictable but utterly danceable.

Kinky Star, Vlasmarkt 9, www.kinkystar.be. *Check website for events and times. Map 3, D7, p254* Run to fund one of Belgium's best indie labels, this Tardis-like place has two stages for live gigs and several DJs a week. The music is quintessentially Ghent: cool, alternative, but always dancefloor-friendly.

Video, Oude Beestenmarkt 7, **T** 09-330 8006. *Tue-Sat 2000-late. Map 3, F8, p254* People in Ghent don't dance much, apparently, but they do in this buzzing boutique bar, with Dan Flavin-style panels of coloured light on one wall and upbeat, uncomplicated music. Live bands on Wednesday, DJs Thursday to Saturday.

Arts and entertainment

Fittingly for a city whose inhabitants see themselves as the heirs of Rubens, Antwerp is the epicentre of the dynamic Flemish arts scene, with world-class contemporary choreographers and classical musicians, as well as a healthy rock and alternative scene, partly inspired by the success of dEUS. Ghent keeps pace thanks to the superb Vooruit arts centre and a huge student population, who contribute to the city's position as a fixture on the European gig circuit.

Venues in both cities tend to be multi-purpose, but there are specialized spaces, too – Ghent's Logos Tetraëder, devoted to newer-than-new music, is a striking example. Unlike many cities, Antwerp has an extensive summer arts programme; Ghent, meanwhile, gives its all for the Gentse Feesten, then pretty much shuts down in August. For information and reservations in Antwerp, visit Prospekta, Grote Markt 13, T 03-203 9585. You can also buy tickets at Fnac, Groenplaats 31, T 03-231 2056, www.fnac.be, or from De Ticketlijn, T 0900 00311, or from abroad, T +32 7034 4304.

Cinema

Belgian cinema has been doing pretty well of late, with the Dardenne brothers winning two Palmes d'Or at Cannes since 1999; but as with everything in this complex country, Belgian is not the same as Flemish. No doubt to the dismay of the Dutch-speakers, francophone directors have been making most of the international running: think of famous Belgian films in recent years and you'll probably come up with *Man Bites Dog*, *The Sexual Life of the Belgians*, *Toto the Hero* and *Rosetta*, all of which were in French.

This may well be down to numbers: a movie made in French has a far greater potential audience than one in Dutch, so is more likely to get international distribution, as well as a Cannes spot. Still, there's no lack of Flemish talent: Frank Van Passel won plaudits for his debut feature, the skewed love story *Manneken Pis*, and for 2002's Elsschot adaptation *Villa des Roses*, with Julie Delpy and Timothy West; Stijn Coninx's powerful *Daens*, about a priest's struggle against poverty in turn-of-the-century Flanders, was Oscar-nominated in 1993; Patrice Toye's *Rosie* is a dark, disturbing teenage rites-of-passage drama; and Dominique Deruddere has a wry and somehow quintessentially Belgian take on life, love and our obsession with celebrity. The daddy of all Flemish directors is the cult hero Harry Kumel, best known for 1971's psych-horror *Malperthuis*, with Orson Welles and more than a hint of surrealism.

Flanders' greatest contribution to European cinema, however, may be the Kinepolis multiplex chain, which moved from humble beginnings in provincial Harelbeke to the development of the first 'megaplex', a 25-screen whopper in Brussels. With state-of-the-art complexes across Europe, from Poznan to Granada, it's a big international player.

! For listings, pick up *Zone 03* (Antwerp) or *Zone 09* (Ghent), or *Week Up* (www.weekup.be) in both cities.

Venues

Cartoons, Kaasstraat 4-6, Antwerp, **T** 03-232 9632, www.cartoons-cinema. be. *Map 2, C3, p252* Art-house cinema just off the Grote Markt, with retrospective seasons and one-off showings of classic films.

Film Museum, Waalse Kaai 47, Antwerp, **T** 03-233 8571. *Map 1, F1, p250* US and European classics, world cinema and new talents.

Metropolis, Groenendaalaan 394, Antwerp, **T** 03-554 3600, www.kinepolis.be. The largest and highest-tech, with 24 auditoriums; a little out of town, though.

Sphinx, Sint-Michielshelling 3, Ghent, **T** 09-225 6086. *Map 3, G1, p255* Art-house in the heart of town, with occasional hits amid the more alternative programming. Ace caff, too.

Studio Skoop, Sint-Annaplein 63, Ghent, **T** 09-225 0845, www.studioskoop.be. *Map 3, off K8 (off map), p255* Better Hollywood films and current European releases, southeast of the centre.

Dance

Contemporary dance and ballet find an appreciative audience in Antwerp and Ghent, with regular visits by international names and world-class local choreographers. Belgium's only ballet company, the **Royal Ballet of Flanders**, has a purpose-built venue in 't Eilandje. It has achieved considerable distinction in the classical repertoire, but the new artistic director, Kathryn Bennetts, who worked as a ballet mistress for William Forsythe, has introduced a more contemporary edge – too contemporary for some.

Arts and entertainment

Modern dance is also in rude health in Flanders. The big four are Brussels-based Anne Teresa de Keersmaeker, who burst onto the scene in the early 1980s and whose **Rosas troupe** is among Europe's finest; Wim Vandekeybus, whose high-octane work for the **Ultima Vez** company is spectacularly physical; the controversial Ghent-based collective **Les Ballets C de la B**, whose best-known stars are Alain Platel and Sidi Larbi Cherkaoui, whose work draws on hip-hop styles; and Jan Fabre, the multi-disciplinary giant of the Flemish arts world, whose 2003 *Swan Lake* saw one dancer wearing a live owl on his head, and whose most recent choreography, *The Crying Body*, outraged audiences at Avignon in 2005. Be warned: laced with sex, violence, swearing, scatology and sometimes all four, Flemish modern dance is not for the faint-hearted.

Venues

DeSingel, Desguinlei 25, Antwerp, **T** 03-248 2828, www.desingel. be. *Map 1, off H5 (off map), p250* The city's main cultural venue, with a first-rate international dance programme.

Koninklijk Ballet van Vlaanderen (Royal Ballet of Flanders), Kattendijkdok-Westkaai 16, Antwerp, **T** 03-234 3438, www.koninklijkballetvanvlaanderen. com. *Map 1, C11, p251*

Monty, Montignystraat 5, Antwerp, **T** 03-238 6497, www.monty.be. *Map 1, G1, p250* Experimental theatre and dance.

Vooruit, Sint-Pietersnieuwstraat 23, Ghent, **T** 09-267 2826, www.vooruit.be. *Map 3, off L6 (off map), p255* Belgian and international dance.

! • If you're a jazz fan, the best venues are De Muze, Buster and Hopper (see Bars and clubs, p163).

> ### The beat goes on

Though **2 Many DJs** are the country's best-known dance act, they're only the latest of Belgium's pioneering electronic musicians. It's often said that Belgians invented techno, and while that's a complex debate, there's no doubt that New Beat, or 'Belgian body beat', had a huge influence in the mid-1980s. The brutally minimalistic beats of **Front 242** laid the foundations for industrial music – the band's Richard 23 formed the **Revolting Cocks** with Ministry's Al Jourgenson – while **Neon Judgement** served up compelling Suicide-tinged techno-goth tunes. Hardcore ravers will have fond memories (or then again, possibly not) of the **Lords of Acid** and **Praga Khan** (*Injected with a Poison*); contemporary hedonists should look out for the **Dewaeles** and their spiritual cousins, **The Glimmers** (who famously segued Frankie Knuckles and, er, Hall & Oates).

Music (pop, rock and dance)

If your understanding of Belgian pop begins and ends with **Plastic Bertrand**, then you need to rewind to 1994, and the advent of **dEUS**, who became instant indie heroes thanks to the violin-driven art-rock of their single *Suds and Soda*. Relieved of the need to apologise for their birthplace, Flemish bands have flourished ever since: dEUS remain mainstays of the Antwerp scene, while Ghent's most famous outfit are **Soulwax**, aka **2 Many DJs**, aka the Dewaele brothers.

The debut dEUS album, *Worst Case Scenario*, is quirky, infectious rock with experimental edges and a warped bluesy feel; *In a Bar Under the Sea*, *The Ideal Crash* and *Pocket Revolution* are also worth a listen. Of the spin-offs, check out the alt-pastoral **Zita Swoon** and any project involving Mauro Pawlowski, whose **Evil Superstars** anthem

Satan Is in My Ass is a contender for best song title ever; in typical Antwerp style, the tourist office asked him to write them a jingle.

Soulwax's breakthrough record was *Much Against Everyone's Advice*, an MTV-friendly mix-and-match of influences from Prince to Black Sabbath, but their best work has been under the moniker 2 Many DJs: they're matchless musical magpies, as anyone who's heard their Christina Aguilera/Strokes *Genie in a Bottle* mash-up will know.

The biggest buzz at the moment surrounds **Millionaire**, who are tipped for international stardom on the back of their latest album, *Paradisiac* – a monumental slab of stoner rock produced by Josh 'Queens of the Stone Age' Homme. They've toured with the Foo Fighters and Muse, but headlining status can't be far away.

Venues

Though there's a thriving local scene, Antwerp is not really on the international circuit: most British and US acts play in Brussels or student-heavy Ghent. But that gives you even less excuse not to check out some Flemish bands…

Charlatan, Ghent, see p172. *Map 3, D7, p254*

Frontline, Ghent, see p172.

Hof ter Lo, Noordersingel 30, Antwerp, **T** 03-543 9030, www.ccluchtbal.org. *Map 1, off B12, p251* Rock venue just outside the ring, east of the centre. Affiliated to the Luchtbal cultural centre (Columbiastraat 8), which stages jazz gigs.

Kaaiman, Antwerp, see p168. *Map 1, C12, p251*

Kinky Star, Ghent, see p176. *Map 3, D7, p254*

Petrol, Antwerp, see p171. *Map 1, off F1 (off map), p250*

Sportpaleis, Schijnpoortweg 119, Antwerp, **T** 0900 450 0045, www.sportpaleis.be. *Map 1, off A11, p251* Tickets **T** 070 345345. Hulking megavenue on the fringes of town.

Vooruit, Sint-Pietersnieuwstraat 23, Ghent, **T** 09-267 2826, www.vooruit.be. *Map 3, off L6 (off map), p255* See also p176.

Zuiderpershuis, Antwerp, see p81. *Map 2, H1, p252* World music.

Music (opera and classical)

Music flourished in Flanders during its Renaissance heyday, so it's no surprise that early music is a particular strength here, with world-class performers and conductors in abundance. Paul Van Nevel, the leader of the **Huelgas Ensemble**, is fanatical about Flemish polyphony, and is forever unearthing lost medieval gems. Bach expert Sigiswald Kuijken helped reinvent violin technique in the late 1960s, and his period-instrument ensemble, **La Petite Bande**, are formidable exponents of French and Italian baroque music. Though their repertoire is not limited to any period, Philippe Herreweghe's **Collegium Vocale Gent** are famed for their mastery of the German baroque; Jos Van Immerseel's orchestra, **Anima Eterna**, apply the historical performance practices of early musicians to 19th-century giants such as Schubert or Beethoven.

Rivals in so many regards, Antwerp and Ghent have at least one thing in common: their opera company. The **Vlaamse Opera** (Flemish Opera: Antwerp building closed for restoration until early 2007) was established in 1989 and performs at the opera houses of each city. It focuses on up-and-coming international talents, and on directors with a contemporary vision: David McVicar, Robert Carsen, Willy Decker and the notorious Catalan shock merchant Calixto Bieito. Italian Giovanni Batistelli is the composer in residence, producing one new opera per season. With tickets starting at just €7, it's not surprising productions sell out fast.

Venues

Several of Antwerp's churches are used for recitals and concerts, including **Carolus Borromeus** and **Sint-Pauluskerk**.

Concert Hall De Bijloke, Jozef Kluyskensstraat 2, Ghent, **T** 09-233 6878, www.debijloke.be. *Map 3, off L2 (off map), p255* Top Flemish orchestras and ensembles, sometimes with world-class musicians (Leif Ove Andsnes, Academie für Alte Musik Berlin).

DeSingel, Desguinlei 25, Antwerp, **T** 03-248 2828, www.desingel. be. *Map 1, off H5, p250* Big names from Belgium and beyond.

De Vlaamse Opera, Frankrijklei 3, Antwerp *(Map 2, D10, p253)*, and Schouwburgstraat 3, Ghent *(Map 3, K3, p255)*, **T** 070-2202022, www.vlaamseopera.be (online ticketing).

Kapel Centrum Elzenveld, Lange Gasthuisstraat 45, Antwerp, **T** 03-229 1880. *Map 2, G6, p252* Atmospheric setting for high-quality early-music recitals and lunchtime chamber music.

Kolveniershof, Kolveniersstraat 20, Antwerp, **T** 03-658 6886. *Map 2, E8, p253* Lunchtime concerts in a marvellous building.

Koningin Elisabethzaal, Koningin Astridplein 26, Antwerp, **T** 03-203 5622, www.elisabethzaal.be. *Map 2, E12, p253* Modern venue hosting regular concerts by the Flanders Philharmonic and the Flemish Radio Orchestra, as well as musicals and pop.

Logos Tetraëder, Bomastraat 26-28, Ghent, **T** 09-223 8089, www.logosfoundation.org. *Map 3, off A8 (off map), p254* Ultra-contemporary classical, computerized and experimental music in a purpose-built venue, the Tetrahedron.

Arts and entertainment

Sint-Augustinuskerk, Kammenstraat 73, Antwerp, **T** 03-202 4660. *Map 2, F5, p252* Deconsecrated baroque church, now used for early-music performances.

Vooruit, Sint-Pietersnieuwstraat 23, Ghent, **T** 09-267 2826, www.vooruit.be. *Map 3, off L6 (off map), p255* See also p176.

Theatre

Many of the more experimental companies (**Needcompany**, **Victoria**, Jan Fabre's **Troubleyn**) blur the boundaries between dance, theatre and musical, helping to overcome the language barrier. Ghent has an English-language theatre company, **Belusa**.

Venues

Arenbergschouwburg, Arenbergstraat 28, Antwerp, **T** 070 222192, www.arenbergschouwburg.be. *Map 2, F7, p253* Big, ugly modern theatre that also hosts variety, cabaret, jazz and pop gigs.

DeSingel, Desguinlei 25, Antwerp, **T** 03-248 2828, www.desingel.be. *Map 1, off H5 (off map), p250* Avant-garde international productions.

Het Toneelhuis, Komedieplaats 18, Antwerp, **T** 03-224 8844, www.toneel huis.be. *Map 2, F7, p253* Based in the beautiful Bourla theatre with a repertoire spanning classic and contemporary works.

NTGent, Sint-Baafsplein 17, Ghent, **T** 09-225 0101, www.ntgent.be. *Map 3, G5, p255* The city's flagship theatre company.

Minardschouwburg, Walpoortstraat 15, Ghent, **T** 09-265 8830, www.minard.be. *Map 3, L6, p255*

Almost every Belgian town has its own festival, and Antwerp and Ghent are no exceptions: hardly a week passes by without a special event of one kind or another, many of them free. Even in the sleepy summer, the Zomer van Antwerpen ensures there's plenty for locals and visitors to do, while Ghent gives itself to a 10-day orgy of culture and consumption, the Gentse Feesten. The more high-minded among you might prefer the Festival of Flanders (Festival van Vlaanderen), which brings world-renowned musicians to Ghent in September, after an August early-music extravaganza in Antwerp. In Antwerp, alternative street parties bring an appropriate edge to this countercultural city.

January

De Nachten (late Jan) Alternative multimedia event at DeSingel, Antwerp (see p181), with rock, avant-jazz and spoken-word gigs.

February

Proximus Diamond Games (mid-Feb) International women's tennis championship at the Sportpaleis, Antwerp, with a gold and diamond racket for anyone who wins three times in a row.

Café Cultuur (late Feb) Multi-disciplinary festival at the Bourla theatre, Antwerp: DJs, comedians, poets.

April

Time Festival (second half Apr) Dance, music theatre and installations, Ghent (www.timefestival.be).

COURTisane Festival (late Apr) Short films and videos at the Vooruit, Ghent (www.courtisane.be).

May

Sinksenfoor (May-Jul) Extensive funfair on the Vlaamse and Waalse Kaais, Antwerp.

Carillon concerts (May-Sep, Mon 2000) Antwerp.

June

Antwerp Fashion Academy Show (mid-Jun) Join international fashion's movers and shakers as they search for the next successors to the Antwerp Six. Booking essential (www.modenatie.com).

Beer Passion (late Jun) Beer tasting on the Groenplaats, Antwerp, with more than 100 varieties (www.beerpassion.com).

July

Zomer van Antwerpen (Jul-Aug) Summer cultural festival, with local and international artists at venues and unusual locations across town. Includes several free concerts (www.zomervanantwerpen.be).

International organ festivals (Jul-Sep) A series of concerts at the cathedrals in Antwerp (www.akc-orgel.be) and Ghent (www.gentsorgelcentrum.be).

Guerilla (early Jul) Alternative street festival on Muntplein, Antwerp (www.guerilla.be).

Polé Polé (early Jul) Youth music on the Linkeroever, Antwerp.

Sfinks (end Jul) World music in Boechout, near Antwerp.

August

Antwerp Kermis (15 Aug) City festival in honour of Antwerp's patron saint, the Virgin Mary. Includes *Antwerp Zing* ("everyone joins in singing"), which ends with the dialect anthem *Antwâarpe*.

Patershol Festival (mid-Aug) Neighbourhood festival in Ghent, with music, markets and lots of street food (www.patershol.org).

Jazz Middelheim (second half Aug) Open-air international jazz in the Middelheim sculpture park, Antwerp (www.jazzmiddelheim.be).

Laus Polyphoniae (late Aug). World-class early-music concerts in venues across Antwerp; part of the Festival of Flanders.

▶ 240-hour party people

For 10 days from the middle of July, Ghent becomes a riot of music, dance, street theatre and puppetry – and a lot of drinking – during the **Gentse Feesten** (www.gentsefeesten.be). The event's origins date from 1843, when the city authorities, fed up with the disruptive effect on the workforce of the city's many neighbourhood fairs, decided to amalgamate them all into one vast bender.

By the late 1960s, the event was in an apparently terminal decline, but the efforts of the Trefpunt cultural organization helped kick-start it in the 1970s, and now it's one of the world's biggest outdoor events. In addition to the free concerts and performances at impromptu stages across the city, bars such as Charlatan and Kinky Star organize several gigs a night, there's an international jazz festival at the Bijloke (www.bluenotefestival.com), and the Vooruit and the ICC host **10 Days Off**, Europe's biggest dance-music festival, with an incredible line-up of superstar DJs and artists (www.10daysoff.be).

One word of warning: the city is packed for the duration, so book well in advance if you're planning to stay. Some locals think the best time to visit is just before the Feesten itself, when the pre-party buzz is at its highest.

Meeting of Styles (late Aug) International graffiti and hip-hop festival on Sint-Andriesplaats, Antwerp (www.meetingofstyles.com).

September

Festival of Flanders (Sep-Oct) International artists congregate in Ghent for magisterial concerts (www.festival-van-vlaanderen.be).

Laundry Day (first half Sep) Funk, house and drum'n'bass DJs, and street parades, in Sint-Andries or Eilandje (www.laundryday.be).

October

Night of the Proms (Oct-Dec) Student festival (but open to all), with pop, rock and classical concerts at the Sportpaleis, Antwerp (www.notp.com).

Flanders International Film Festival (mid-Oct) Ghent hosts the biggest cinema event in the Benelux (www.filmfestival.be).

November

Jewish Festival (end Nov) Jewish music festival at the Zuiderpershuis, Antwerp (www.zuiderpershuis.be).

December

Christmas Markets Groenplaats, Antwerp; Sint-Baafsplein, Ghent.

Open-air ice rinks Grote Markt, Antwerp; Emile Braunplein, Ghent.

Snow and Ice Sculpture (Dec-Jan) Vlaamse and Waalse Kaais, Antwerp (www.ijssculptuur.com).

New Year's Eve Fireworks on the Scheldt, Antwerp.

Shopping

Antwerp's pedigree as a retail paradise can be traced to the 16th century, when it was known as *de triomfelycke coopstad* ('triumphant shopping city'). That certainly rings true today, as the worldwide popularity of the Antwerp Six and their successors has made the city a high-fashion hub to rival Paris or Milan. Local designers are clustered in Sint-Andries, in particular on Nationalestraat and Lombardenvest. For street styles, vintage and grungy alternative shops, mooch over to nearby Kammenstraat; for international fashion houses, the Latin Quarter is the place.

Even if you're not a dedicated follower of fashion, you'll find it hard to come away empty-handed: Kloosterstraat has a score of splendid antiques and retro design stores, the Zuid is full of super-swish contemporary design shops, and you'll find fantastic delis and food emporia all over town.

Most shops are open Monday to Saturday from 1000 to 1900; the sales are in January and July. Only unusual opening hours are listed below.

Antwerp

Accessories and jewellery

Anne Zellen, Kammenstraat 47, **T** 03-226 8970. *Closed Mon.*
Map 2, E4, p252 Classical, extravagant and ultra-romantic
jewellery: baroque-style pendants, earrings and wedding rings
with hidden messages or hearts.

Boon, Lombardenvest 2 4, **T** 03 233 3387. *Map 2, E5, p252*
Old-fashioned glove specialist with an atmospheric 1930s interior.

Christa Reniers, Vrijdagmarkt 8, **T** 03-233 2602, www.christa
reniers.com. *Tue-Thu 1200-1830, Fri-Sat 1030-1300 and 1400-1830.*
Map 2, E4, p252 Sober, sometimes chunky designer jewellery.

Cocodrillo, Schuttershofstraat 9, **T** 03-233 2093. *Map 2, F7, p253*
Shoes for men, women and children: Branquinho, Margiela,
Demeulemeester, Van Noten, AF Vandervorst, Prada.

Elsa, Nationalestraat 147, **T** 03-226 8454. *Map 2, H3, p252*
Upmarket footwear emporium: Angelo Figus, Costume National
and Belgium's Nathalie Verlinden.

Hilde van Belleghem, Nationalestraat 14, **T** 03-226 8566.
Mon-Tue, Sat 1400-1800, Thu-Fri from 1100. Map 2, E4, p252
Jewellery in unusual sculpted shapes (wonky circles and suchlike),
as well as engagement and wedding rings.

Maison de Parfum, Grote Markt 19, **T** 03-288 5388,
www.parfumeur.be. *Wed-Mon 1100-1900. Map 2, C3, p252*
Perfumes are tailor-made and the free consultation process is
fun in itself.

Nadine Wijnants, Nationalestraat 14, **T** 03-231 7515; Klooster-straat 26, T 03-226 4569, www.nadinewijnants.be. *Closed Mon. Map 2, E4/E2, p252* Delicate, almost ethereal jewellery.

Nico Taeymans, Korte Gasthuisstraat 13, **T** 03-231 6343. *Mon 1200-1800, Tue-Sat 1000-1800. Map 2, E6, p252* Chunky gold and silver jewellery, designed by a former dock worker.

Ridder & Borzée, Groendalstraat 11, **T** 03-294 3844. *Mon 1200-1800, Tue-Sat 1000-1800. Map 2, E6, p252* Stylish engagement and wedding rings.

Wouters & Hendrix, Lange Gasthuisstraat 13, **T** 03-231 6242. *Map 2, F6, p252* Witty jewellery, including cufflinks for men.

Zappa, Kammenstraat 74, **T** 03-227 5440. *Mon and Wed-Fri 1300-1800, Sat 1200-1800. Map 2, F5, p252* Streetwise shoes and trainers. Good place to pick up clubbing information.

Antiques and interiors

There are many places to browse on Kloosterstraat and Leopoldstraat. For the locations of other antiques shops, visit www.antiquairs-antwerpen.be and www.antiquesantwerp.com.

Art galleries

Maes & Matthys, Pourbusstraat 3, **T** 0478-485031. *Wed-Sun 1400-1800. Map 1, F1, p250*

! If you're looking for that ring, steer clear of Pelikaanstraat and head for Diamondland (see p72), where there's a bespoke service. Contact them in advance to discuss your requirements.

Micheline Szwajcer, Verlatstraat 14, **T** 03-237 1127. *Map 1, F1, p250* Quality gallery selling international contemporary art.

Stella Lohaus, Vlaamse Kaai 47, **T** 03-248 0871. *Map 1, F1, p250*

Szymon, Steenhouwersvest 33, **T** 03-231 0442. *Map 2, E3, p252* Prints and paintings by big names such as Panamarenko and Pierre Alechinsky.

Books and magazines

Boekenmarkt de Markies, Melkmarkt 17, **T** 03-289 4225. *Sun-Thu 1100-1830, Fri-Sat 1100-1900. Map 2, D5, p252* The ground-floor International Magazine Store is a good place to catch up on home news.

Copyright, Nationalestraat 28, **T** 03-232 3416. *Tue-Sat 1100-1830, Sun 1400-1800. Map 2, F4, p252* The ModeNatie's shop stocks trendy tomes on art, architecture, fashion and photography.

De Groene Waterman, Wolstraat 7, **T** 03-232 9394. *Map 2, C5, p252* Unashamedly intellectual store, once voted the best bookshop in Flanders.

Fnac, Groenplaats 31, **T** 03-213 5611. *Map 2, D5, p252* Well-stocked chain store with a good CD section.

Mekanik Strip, Sint-Jacobsmarkt 73, **T** 03-234 2347, www.mekanik-strip.be. *Map 2, C9, p253* Flanders' leading comic-strip specialist.

Standaard Boekhandel, Huidevetterstraat 57, **T** 03-231 0773. *Map 2, F6, p252* Flanders' main books chain; plenty of books about Antwerp, in several languages.

Fashion

Ann Demeulemeester, Verlatstraat 38, **T** 03-216 0133. *Map 1, F2, p250* The Antwerp Sixer's flagship store is as minimal as her celebrated monochrome designs. Paradise for *Horses*-era Patti Smith wannabes, though she does colour just as brilliantly.

Astoria, Nationalestraat 11, **T** 03-233 7574. *Map 2, E4, p252* Rudy De Boyser, Kaat Tilley, Sandwich, Fun Factory.

Baby Beluga, Volkstraat 1, **T** 03-289 9060. *1100-1830. Closed Sun and Tue. Map 2, H3, p252* Feminine, flowing, flowery clothes and upmarket accessories for women.

Christoph Broich, Steenhouwersvest 28, **T** 03-770 8653. *Wed-Sat 1100-1830. Map 2, E3, p252* Creative designer threads and safety-pinned sunglasses by another Fashion Academy graduate.

Clinic, De Burburestraat 5, **T** 03-248 6911, www.clinicantwerp.com. *Mon-Sat 1000-1830, Sun 1300-1700. Map 1, F1, p250* Cavernous shop selling trendy jeans, streetwear and casual clothes – Dirk Bikkembergs, Paul Smith Jeans, G-Star, Diesel and the like.

Closing Date, Korte Gasthuisstraat 15, **T** 03-232 8722. *Map 2, E6, p252* Upmarket clothes for clubbers and connoisseurs, notably Dsquared2 and Vivienne Westwood.

Episode, Steenhouwersvest 34A, **T** 03-234 341. *Closed Sat mornings. Map 2, E3, p252* Vintage designer wear and accessories.

Fish and Chips, Kammenstraat 36-38, **T** 03-227 0824, www.fishandchips.be. *Map 2, E4, p252* The epicentre of Antwerp's clothing counterculture: hilarious window displays and three floors of ultracool jeans, trainers, clubwear and skatewear.

Francis, Steenhouwersvest 14, **T** 03-288 9433. *Map 2, E3, p252* Vintage and second-hand designer clobber.

Garde-robe Nationale, Nationalestraat 141, **T** 03-234 2243. *Map 2, F4, p252* Tommy Fjorside, Sportmax, Just in Case.

Harry Beaver, Kammenstraat 34, **T** 03-227 4601. *Mon-Fri 1200-1800, Sat 1100-1800. Map 2, E4, p252* Skatewear.

Het Modepaleis, Nationalestraat 16, **T** 03-470 2510. *Map 2, E4, p252* An imposing 19th-century corner house is the showcase for Dries Van Noten's fabulously flattering creations.

Hit, Kammenstraat 43, **T** 03-226 0231. *Map 2, E4, p252* Hipster kit.

Labels Inc, Aalmoezenierstraat 4, **T** 03-232 6056, www.labelsinc.be. *Mon-Tue, Thu-Sat 1100-1800, Wed 1400-1800. Map 2, G4, p252* Recent designer and second-hand clothes, including Belgian labels.

Louis, Lombardenvest 2, **T** 03-232 9872. *Map 2, E4, p252* The first shop to stock designs by the Antwerp Six, and still at the cutting edge of contemporary fashion. Most of the labels are Belgian, but they deign to stock the uber-desirable creations of Nicolas Ghesquière for Balenciaga.

Naughty I, Kammenstraat 65-67, **T** 03-213 3590, www.naughty.be. *Map 2, F5, p252* Way-out second-hand clothes and clubwear.

Stephan Schneider, Reyndersstraat 53, **T** 03-226 2614. *Map 2, D4, p252* Flagship store for another Fashion Academy graduate: witty, unusual designs and fine fabrics for men and women.

Vegas, Kammenstraat 57, **T** 03-289 3368. *Mon 1300-1800, Tue-Sat 1100-1830. Map 2, F4, p252* Knowingly kitsch retro vintage clothes.

Shopping

Verlaine, Kasteelpleinstraat 34, **T** 03-237 1660, www.romysmits.com. *Thu-Sat 1400-1800, or by appointment.* *Map 1, F3, p250* Vintage haute couture.

Veronique Branquinho, Nationalestraat 73, **T** 03-233 6616. *Map 1, D3, p250* Sober, sculpted clothes by one of the most high-profile Fashion Academy graduates.

Verso, Lange Gasthuisstraat 9-11, **T** 03-226 9292, www.verso.be. *Map 2, F6, p250* Chic store in an old bank: Armani, Helmut Lang and Donna Karan, as well as Belgian design.

Walter, Sint Antoniusstraat 12, **T** 03-213 2644. *Mon 1300-1830, Tue-Sat from 1100. Map 2, F4, p252* Antwerp Sixer Walter Van Beirendonck's flagship store is worth a visit for the futurist industrial decor alone. As well as the big man's main line, it stocks beautiful prints by another Antwerp Sixer, Dirk Van Saene.

Food and drink

For details of where to buy exotic world foods and spices, pick up the Winkelend Noord brochure from the tourist office.

Belgium Beers, Suikerrui 34, **T** 03-226 6853. *Daily 1000-2000.* *Map 2, C3, p252*

Bio-Dynamische Bakerij, Volkstraat 17, **T** 03-216 0042. *Mon-Sat 0800-1800. Map 1, F2, p250* Organic bakery.

Burie, Korte Gasthuisstraat 3, **T** 03-232 3688, www.chobel.be. *0900-1830. Map 2, E6, p252* Top-notch chocolatier. As well as peerless pralines, it offers pots of chocolate mussels, diamonds and hands.

Del Rey, Appelmanstraat 5, **T** 0470 28 61. *Mon-Sat, 0900-1830. Map 2, E11, p253* A long-established tearoom and chocolate haunt.

Goossens, Korte Gasthuisstraat 31, **T** 03-226 0791. *Map 2, E6, p252* Tiny old-fashioned bakery, famous for its raisin bread (once donated to the condemned by a benevolent citizen, see p45).

Kleinblatt, Provinciestraat 206, **T** 03-234 3535. *Map 1, F8, p251* Kosher bakery with great apple tarts.

Markets

Falconplein, www.antwerpen.be/schipperskwartier. *First Sun of the month, 1000-1600. Map 1, A4, p250* Organic market.

Kerstmarkt, Grote Markt. *2nd week Dec. Map 2, C4, p252* Christmas market.

Lijnwaadmarkt. *Sat 0900-1700, Easter-Oct. Map 2, C5, p252* Antiques, brocante.

Rubensmarkt, Grote Markt. *Aug 15. Map 2, C4, p252* Folkloric market held in honour of the city's patron, the Madonna. Lots of gifts for mothers on sale.

Sint-Jansvliet. *Sun 0900-1700. Map 2, D3, p252* Flea market.

Theaterplein. *Sat 0800-1600. Map 2, G8, p253* Ethnic food.

Theaterplein. *Sun 0830-1300. Map 2, G8, p253* Bird market.

Vrijdagmarkt. *Fri from 0900. Map 2, E4, p252* Lively open-air auction.

Shopping

Music

Bam Bam, Nationalestraat 63, **T** 03-288 1077. *Tue, Wed and Sat, 1100-1800, Thu-Fri 1100-2000. Map 2, F4, p252* Zambian hip-hop, Latino rap, ragga and drum'n'bass.

R.E.P.L.A.Y., Lange Koepoortstraat 78, **T** 03-226 0327. *Mon-Sat 1100-1800, Sun 1400-1800. Map 2, B5, p252* A great selection of second-hand music books and sheet music.

Tune Up, Korte Nieuwstraat 9, **T** 03-226 8411. *Wed-Sat 1100-1800. Map 2, C5, p252* One of the best second-hand vinyl stores in town; all genres, but especially strong on electronica.

Vinyl, Aalmoezenierstraat 27, **T** 03-213 0059. *Tue-Fri 1100-1830, Sat 1200-1900. Map 2, G4, p252* Second-hand vinyl and CDs, from classical and jazz to indie and new wave.

Ghent

Antiques and interiors

Fallen Angels, Jan Breydelstraat 29-31, **T** 09-223 9415. *Daily 1300-1800. Map 3, D2, p254* Bric-a-brac, old postcards, vintage toys.

Kloskanthuis, Korenlei 3, **T** 09-223 6093. *Tue-Sun 1000-1800. Map 3, E2, p254* Lace and linen made in traditional fashion, as they have been here since the 1880s.

Books

De Schaar, Serpentstraat 28, **T** 09-223 7371, www.deschaar.com. *Mon-Sat 1200-1830. Map 3, D5, p254* A treasure trove of comics.

Fashion and accessories

Annie B, Sint-Pietersnieuwstraat 84, **T** 09-224 2146. *Mon-Fri 1030-1230, 1400-1730, Sat 1030-1200. Map 3, off L6 (off map), p255* Good-quality second-hand clothes.

Bernard Gavilan, Sint-Pietersnieuwstraat 1, **T** 09-233 5761. *Mon-Sat 1100-1830. Map 3, off L6 (off map), p255* The coolest vintage clothes in town, perfect for throwing together that shabby-chic student look.

Boomerang, Kortrijksepoortstraat, **T** 09-225 3707. *Tue-Sat 1400-1815. Map 3, off L3 (off map), p255* Hip second-hand clothes store.

Den Oorcussen, Vrijdagmarkt 7, **T** 09-233 0765. *Tue-Sat 1030-1800. Map 3, D5, p254* Upmarket clothes for women by the Antwerp Six and more recent graduates of the Fashion Academy.

Obius, Meerseniersstraat 4, **T** 09-233 8269, www.obius.be. *Mon 1330-1800, Tue-Sat 1030-1830. Map 3, C4, p254* Shoes and clothes by Belgian and international designers: Branquinho, Bikkembergs, Prada, AF Vandevorst, Van Noten.

Food and drink

Bloch, Veldstraat 60, **T** 09-225 7085. *Map 3, I2, p255* Delicious cakes and pastries, including *mastellen* with cinnamon.

De Hopduvel, Coupure Links 625, **T** 09-225 2068. *1000-1230, 1330-1830. Map 3, off J1, p255* Beers and matching glasses.

Michel Peeters, Hoornstraat 9, **T** 09-225 6968. *Map 3, H3, p255* One of the best cheese shops in Belgium (famously, it's next to a sock shop).

Markets

Bij Sint Jacobs. *Fri-Sun 0800-1300. Map 3, D6, p254* Flea market.

Groentenmarkt. *Mon-Fri 0700-1300, Sat 0700-1700. Map 3, E3, p254* Fruit and vegetables.

Kouter. *0700-1300. Map 3, J4, p255* Flowers.

Oude Beestenmarkt. *Sun 0700-1300. Map 3, F8, p254* Small animals and poultry.

Sint-Michielsplein. *Sun morning. Map 3, G1, p255* Food.

Sint-Veerleplein. *Sat-Sun 1000-1800. Map 3, D3, p254* Handicrafts.

Vrijdagmarkt. *Sun 0700-1300. Map 3, D5, p254* Birds.

Music

City Beatz, Lammerstraat 4a 9000, **T** 09-234 3428. *Mon-Fri 1100-1900. Map 3, off L6, p255* Hip-hop and R'n'B.

Fried Chicken Records, Nederkouter 47, **T** 09-223 1627. *Map 3, L2, p255* Hip-hop, funk and drum'n'bass.

Music Mania, Bagattenstraat 197, **T** 09-225 6815. *Mon-Fri 1100-1900, Sat 1100-1800. Map 3, off L6, p255* Biggest vinyl shop in Ghent.

Vinyl Kitchen, Lange Violettestraat 160, **T** 09-474 25 55 06. *Wed- Fri 1200-1930, Sat 1300-1930. Map 3, off K8 (off map), p255* Rock and soul.

A Catholic region with strong Dutch influences, Flanders could swing either way in terms of its attitude to homosexuality. Thankfully, Antwerp and Ghent are both tolerant, gay-friendly cities, and if the scene here is less in your face than Amsterdam's, it's still vibrant enough to attract crowds from northern France and the Netherlands. Same-sex marriage is legal in Belgium, and adoption by gay couples is being discussed in parliament. The first gay associations in Flanders sprung up in Ghent, which was the first Belgian town to produce a gay city map. Antwerp city council has a department of emancipation and non-discrimination, which publishes a free guide for gays, *Antwerpen Anders*. With gay-friendly establishments scattered across the city, there's no gay district as such, though Van Schoonhovenstraat and the Stadspark are cruising zones. Ghent has little in the way of an organized gay scene, but its strong student community and liberal tradition mean gays are welcome everywhere.

Associations

Atthis, Geuzenstraat 27, Antwerp, **T** 03-216 3737, www.atthis.be.
Map 1, F2, p250 Lesbian association with a meeting room and
library. It organizes walks, cycling and social and cultural events.

Casa Rosa, Kammerstraat 22, Ghent, **T** 09-269 2812,
www.casarosa.be. *Map 3, D5, p254* This café is a Holebi centre,
with information about what's on in Ghent and beyond.

Enig Verschil, Postbus 144, Antwerp, **T** 0496-997098,
www.enigverschil.be. Antwerp group for Holebis (a Dutch term
used to encompass gay men, lesbians and bisexuals) under 26.
Meets Wednesday at De Groene Waterman bookshop (see p197).

Het Roze Huis, Café Den Draak, Draakplaats 1, Antwerp, **T** 03-288
0084, www.hetrozehuis.be. *Information and help service Thu 1700-
2100. Map 1, G9, p251* The Pink House is an umbrella organization
for gays, lesbians and bisexuals, with its headquarters above the
café. It publishes a quarterly magazine, *De Magneet* (in Dutch). This
building is also home to **Active Company**, **T** 0477-510305,
www.activecompany.be, a Holebi (see below) sports group with
more than 400 members, one in four of whom are women.

Holebifederatie, Kammerstraat 22, Ghent, **T** 09-223 6929,
www.holebifederatie.be. *Weekdays 0900-1200 and 1300-1700.
Map 3, E6, p254* This pan-Flanders association, promoting gay,
lesbian and bisexual rights, publishes a magazine, *ZiZo*
(www.zizo-magazine.be), and runs a helpline, **T** 09-238 2626.

! Van Schoonhovenstraat's collection of gay bars has earned it
the nickname 'Vaseline Street'.

Holebifoon, T 09-238 2626, www.holebifoon.be. *Mon-Sun 1800-2200, Wed 1400-2200.* Ghent-based anonymous helpline for gays, lesbians and bisexuals.

Homo 40 +, Steenbokstraat 15, Antwerp, www.derozerimpel.be. *Map 1, G8, p251* A group for gay men over 40, which meets every second and fourth Friday of the month at the Roze Huis (see p215).

O Radio, Londenstraat 7, Antwerp, **T** 03-727 1070, www.oradio.be. *Map 1, C12, p251* Belgium's first gay radio station. Tune in to 107.0FM to find out what's on in town.

Sensoa, Kipdorpvest 48A, Antwerp, **T** 03-238 6868, www.sensoa.be. *Mon-Fri 0830-1230, 1330-1630. Map 2, D10, p253* Umbrella group for HIV, Aids and buddy groups.

Events

NaviGAYtion, Steenplein, Antwerp, www.navigaytion.be. *Map 2, B3, p252* Huge party (mid-Aug) on and by the water, with party boats, international DJs and fireworks of all kinds.

Bars and cafés

The Boots, Van Aerdstraat 22, Antwerp, **T** 03-233 2136, www.the-boots.com. *Fri-Sat 2230-0500. Map 1, A6, p250* A leather and fetish bar, famous throughout Europe for offering "freedom, fantasy and sex". As the website says, people don't come here for the decor.

Club XL, Van Schoonhovenstraat 40, Antwerp, **T** 03-232 0065. 1800-0600. *Map 2, D12, p253* Men and women.

Hessenhuis, Falconrui 53, Antwerp, **T** 03-231 1356, www.hessen huis.com. *Mon-Tue from 1100, Sat from 1500 and Sun from 1300. Map 2, off A8, p253* Evenings only: at lunch, it's a museum café.

Popi, Plantinkaai 12, Antwerp, **T** 03-238 1530, www.popi.be. *1200-late. Map 2, E2, p252* Cheery, high-energy gay and lesbian bar that welcomes all comers. Bright decor and DJs on Saturday nights.

't Verschil, Minderbroedersrui 42, Antwerp, **T** 03-226 0804, www.verschil.be. *Wed-Sun 1200-1800. Map 2, B6, p252* Gay bookshop and café.

Zone G, Dambruggestraat 174, Antwerp, www.zoneg.be. *Weekdays only, 1230-2200. Map 1, C7, p251* Adult cruising lounge.

In Ghent, the **Casa Rosa**'s bar is the main meeting point (see p207).

Clubs and parties

Red and Blue, Lange Schipperskapelstraat 11, Antwerp, **T** 03-213 0555, www.redandblue.be. *Sat 2300-late. Map 1, A3, p250* Men only. Occasional lesbian nights, called Café de Love.

In Ghent, gay parties are held at **Cocteau**, Palfijnstraat 29; the **Vooruit** (see pp110 and 177); and **Twideoo**, Overpoortstraat 9. The Casa Rosa is the place to pick up details (see p207).

Saunas

Kouros Sauna, Botermelkbaan 50, Antwerp, **T** 03-658 0937. *1300-0100, Sun 1100-late.* For men.

Gay and lesbian

Spa 55, Sanderusstraat 55, Antwerp, **T** 03-238 3137, www.spa55.be. 1300-0000. *Map 1, G3, p250* For men.

Gay-run B&Bs and guesthouses

B+B2000, Van Boendalestraat 8, Antwerp, **T** 03-234 1210, guestrooms.happygays.be *Map 2, C10, p253*

Emperors 48, Keizerstraat 48, Antwerp, **T** 03-228 7337, www.emperors 48.com. *Map 2, C7, p253*

Guesthouse G8, Geulincxstraat 8, Antwerp, **T** 0477-626281/0475-201996, info@gb.be. *Map 1, A6, p250* Gay men only. Has a leather bar.

Mabuhay, Draakstraat 32, Antwerp, **T** 03-290 8815, www.mabuhay.be. *Map 1, G9, p251*

't Katshuis, Grote Pieter Potstraat 18, Antwerp, **T** 0476-206947, www.katshuis.be. *Map 2, C3, p252* A former gay bar.

't Verschil, Minderbroedersrui 42, Antwerp, **T** 03-226 0804, info@verschil.be *Map 2, B6, p252*

Websites

www.gaybelgium.be; www.gaylife.be; www.gaydayz.be.

Though they may not strike you as ideal family destinations, Antwerp and Ghent are both child-friendly cities: youngsters are welcome pretty much everywhere, and people are generally helpful when it comes to such things as shifting buggies on or off trams or trains. You'll find play areas in children's shops and restaurants, some of which have children's menus (usually a choice of pasta, fish fingers or chicken with apple puree) and colouring books. Even those that don't will often allow children to share a dish off the adult menu, or provide smaller portions. There's a dearth of green spaces in both city centres, but there are playgrounds, with parks and recreation centres on the outskirts. During school holidays and festivals, there are often special activities for children in museums and elsewhere. Families should also consider a day trip to Mechelen, which has reinvented itself as a 'Children's Town' (visit www.mechelen.be/kinderstad).

Childcare

National Gezinsbond (Family League) has a list of babysitters. For recommendations, contact Mrs Brughmans, **T** 03-295 7080 or 0476 617952, www.gezinsbond.be. Gail Ryckbosch is an experienced English-speaking babysitter/mother in the Antwerp area, **T** 03-605 5912/0496 892792.

Museums

De Wereld van Kina, Ghent (see p111).

Film Museum, Antwerp (see p83). Sometimes has programmes for children aged 8 and up.

Gravensteen, Ghent (see p107). One for the boys, perhaps: a whole castle for playing knights and dragons, and loads of torture instruments.

Middelheim Sculpture Park, Antwerp, (p95). The marble polar bear is a sure-fire winner.

Steen, Antwerp (see p43). At the Maritime Museum, children can tie nautical knots or try on fishermen's costumes and hats.

Toy Museum, Nekkerspoel, Mechelen, **T** 015-557075, www.speelgoedmuseum.be. *Tue-Sun 1000-1700.* With fine collections of dolls and their houses, toys from around the world (including Sri Lankan percussion instruments), Meccano and Lego, there's plenty to keep adults entertained, and play areas for children of different ages should satisfy even the most reluctant young museumgoer.

Kids

Other sights

Antwerp Zoo, Antwerp (p73).

Aquatopia, Antwerp, (see p74). A bit disappointing for adults, but children love the touch-screen technology, and there's a handy toddlers' play area and several toilets.

Piraten Eiland, Kribbestraat 12, Antwerp, **T** 03-213 5060, www.piraten eiland.info. *Wed 1200-1800, Thu-Fri 0930-1600, Sat-Sun 1100-1800; Jul-Aug, Wed-Sun 1100-1800; Sep, Sat-Sun 1100-1800. €8, or €7 if you're on the Diamond Bus (see p28). Map 1, C12, p251* Ahoy, me hearties! Pirate Island is a sprawling indoor adventure park built around a fully rigged galleon, with two floors of tunnels and slides, a sandpit, a bouncy castle and a cinema room screening pirate-themed movies. Parents can grab a beer while the children play.

Planckendael Wildlife Park, Mechelen, **T** 015-414921, www.planckendael.be. *Jul-Aug 1000-1900; May-Jun, Sep -1800; Mar-Apr, Oct -1730; Nov-Feb -1645. €15, children €9.90.* The breeding ground for Antwerp Zoo offers animals (and children) considerably more room to roam, and has an unforced educational bent, with plenty of hands-on activities and explanations of innovations such as the solar-powered rhino shower. If the animals lose their magic, there's always the treetop walk, a succession of climbing frames and rope ladders that twists through the branches, a good 60 feet up – but parents should accompany younger children, as there's no easy way back. Do as the locals do and bring sandwiches – there are several picnic areas, including one near the monkeys. In summer, the best route from Mechelen to Planckendael is by boat: **Rederij Malinska**, **T** 0477 364820, www.rederijmalinska.be, has half-hourly services from Colomabrug, behind Mechelen's station.

Kids

Technopolis, Technologielaan, Mechelen, **T** 015 342000, www.technopolis.be. *0930-1700. €8.90, children 3-11 €6.40.* A high-tech, hugely interactive museum devoted to the wonders of science, with 261 hands-on exhibits on the human body, water, road safety, domestic appliances, musical instruments, communication and much, much more. The most spectacular attraction is a bike ride on a high wire, a good 30 feet above the floor (before you panic, there's a safety harness).

Sleeping

Many hotels offer free or relatively inexpensive beds to children staying in their parents' room. Many of the bigger hotels have babysitting services. Family-run B&Bs welcome children, especially those of an age to play with the family's own children, in particular **Bed, Bad, Brood** (p130), **Ann, Paul & Kids** (p130), the **Melkhuis** (p132) and **Guesthouse 26** (p125). The following hotels have spacious accommodation for families: **'t Elzenveld** in school holidays (p126), **Astrid Park Plaza** (p127), **Alfa Empire** (p127) and **Ghent River Hotel** (p133). The following B&Bs /guesthouses also have family-friendly apartments or studios: **Brooderie** (p135), **Café Folklore** (p136), **Patine** (p130) and **Ecohuis** (p132).

Eating

Berlin, Antwerp (p146). The playroom at the back is basic, but children seem to love it.

€€ Sensunik, Molenstraat 69, Antwerp, **T** 03-216 0066, www.sensunik.be. *Map 1, G4, p250* Parents dine downstairs on snails, rocket salad, steak, ribs or Mediterranean-style fish, while childminders look after children in the upstairs crèche (they also get a meal, €10 in total).

Other particularly child-friendly restaurants and cafes in Antwerp: **'t Brantyser** (p143), **Noorderterras** (p143), **De 7 Schaken** (p141), **Brasserie du Noord** (p142), **Mata Mata & Pili Pili** (p142), **Sjalot en Schanul** (p144), **Zuiderterras** (p147), **The Bistro** (p146), **Chez Fred** (p148), **Bizzie Lizzie** (p150), **O'Tagine** (p151), **De Broers van Julienne** (p152), **Dansing Chocola** (p166), **Funky Soul Potato** (p152), **L'Entrepot du Congo** (p152), **Bassin** (p153), **Comcarmenne** (p154), **El Warda** (p155), **Wattman** (p155).

In Ghent: **Graaf van Egmond** (p157), **Raj** (p159), **'t Klokhuys** (p159), **De Foyer** (p157), **Avalon** (p159).

Theatre

De Maan Puppet Theatre, Minderbroedersgang 1 and 3, Mechelen, **T** 015 200200, www.demaan.be.

Froe Froe Puppet Theatre, Namenstraat 7, Antwerp, **T** 03-248 7221, www.froefroe.be. *Map 1, off G1, p250*

Fairs and festivals

Gentse Feesten (p191). The children's festival offers dancing, theatre, music and puppetry.

Sinksenfoor (p189). Vast fairground, candyfloss, tack and all.

Zomer van Antwerpen (p190). Outdoor theatre and music for children.

Playgrounds

Antwerp: Sint-Andriesplaats; Kleinkoraalberg; the southern end of the Vlaamse and Waalse Kaais; Munthof; Stadspark.

Ghent: near Vrijdagmarkt, at the end of Bibliotheekstraat; Citadelpark, near Sint-Pietersstation.

Outdoor activities and recreation centres

Bobbejaanland, Olensesteenweg 45, Lichtaart, near Antwerp, **T** 014-557211, www.bobbejaanland.be. Amusement park with thrills aplenty.

De Nekker, Nekkerspoel-Borcht 19, Mechelen, **T** 015-557005, www.denekker.be. 1000-2000, Jul-Aug, -2100. €3, children 6-12 €2.50. This is a huge recreation park with a beach, a playground and all manner of activities: go-carting, minigolf, cycling, table tennis, inline skating and so on. It's also home to **Nekki**, a vast indoor play area for under-12s (*Wed 1230-1930, Sat-Sun 1130-1930, school holidays daily 1130-1930*).

Tivoli, Antwerpsesteenweg 94, Mechelen, **T** 015-206684, www.mechelen.be/tivoli. *Weekends 0830-sunset, weekdays -1700, winter -1600.* Nature education centre with walking trails and a children's farm.

Shopping

Books
De Kleine Prins, Scheldestraat 77, Antwerp, **T** 03-237 9765. *Closed Mon. Map 1, F2, p250* Esoteric and spiritual bookshop that also stocks children's books. **De Verbeelding**, Henegouwenstraat 121, Ghent, **T** 09-225 2148. *Map 3, I5, p255*

Clothes
Cats and Dogs, Nationalestraat 12, Antwerp, **T** 03-213 2840. *Map 2, E4, p252* **De Groene Volk**, Korte Gasthuisstraat 20, Antwerp, **T** 03-234 1847. *Map 2, E6, p252* **Kids on the Dock**,

Vlaamse Kaai 27, **T** 03-237 2259. *Map 1, F1, p250*
Oilily, Schuttershofstraat 26, **T** 03-234 2947. *Map 2, F7, p253*
Prinses op de Erwt, Graaf van Egmontstraat 1, **T** 03-216 4118.
Map 2, H2, p252

Toys
Jojo, Volkstraat 36, Antwerp, **T** 03-216 9626. *Map 1, F2, p250*
Olifant, Leopoldstraat 23, Antwerp, **T** 03-231 6114. *Map 2, G7, p253* **Petit Zsa-Zsa**, Serpenstraat 5, Ghent, **T** 09-224 4574.
Map 3, D5, p254 Unusual gifts and toys with a fashionable feel.

Directory

Airline offices

Antwerp: **VLM**, T 03-285 6868, www.flyvlm.com; **Welcome Air**, www.welcomeair.com. Brussels: **SN Airlines**, www.flysn.be; **Virgin Express**, www.virgin-express.com. Charleroi: **Ryanair**, www.ryanair.com.

Banks and ATMs

Most banks are open Mon-Fri, 0900-1600. There is a shortage of ATMs in Antwerp, with many cash machines for local customers only, but you will find them on Eiermarkt (ground floor of the Boerentoren), halfway down Nationalestraat and on Groenplaats, near the post office. In Ghent, there are ATMs by the Vleeshuis and opposite Sint-Michielskerk. Traveller's cheques and international credit cards are accepted in all major hotels, restaurants and shops.

Bicycle hire

Antwerp: **De Ligfiets**, Steenhouwersvest, **T** 03-293 7456, www.ligfiets.be; **De Windroos**, Steenplein, **T** 03-480 9388; **Fiets-Dokter**, Verschansingstraat 48, **T** 03-237 8254.

Ghent: **Student Bike Rental**, Kattenberg 2, **T** 09-269 1898, www.studentenmobiliteit.be; **Biker**, Steendam 16, **T** 09-224 2903; **De Ligfiets**, Lange Violettestraat 49, **T** 09-223 4496; **Sint-Pietersstation**, Koningin Maria Hendrikaplein, T 09-241 2224.

Car hire

Antwerp: **Avis**, **T** 03-218 9496, www.avis.be, and **Hertz**, **T** 03-239 2921, www.hertz.be, have offices at Antwerp airport; or try **Alfa Car**, Noorderlaan 85, **T** 03-546 4478, www.alfacar.be; **Budget**, Noorderlaan 32, **T** 03-232 3500, www.budget.com; **Europcar**, Plantin en Moretuslei 35, **T** 03-206 7444, www.europcar.be.

Ghent: **Avis**, Kortrijksesteenweg 676-678, **T** 09-222 0053, www.avis.be; **Europcar**, Einde Were 1, **T** 09-226 8126, www.europcar.be; **Hertz**, Nieuwewanderling 76, **T** 09-224 0406, www.hertz.be.

Consulates and embassies
Australian Embassy, Guimardstraat 6-8, Brussels, **T** 02-286 0500; **Canada Honorary Consul**, Sint-Pietersvliet 15, Antwerp, **T** 03-220 0211, www.ambassade-canada.be; **Great Britain Honorary Consul**, p/a Box 580, Groenplaats, Antwerp, **T** 03-213 2125, www.british-embassy.be; **Ireland Honorary Consul**, F Verbiestlaan 38, Edegam, Antwerp, **T** 03-289 0611; **Israel Honorary Consul**, Pelikaanstraat 62, Antwerp, **T** 03-232 5170; **New Zealand Honorary Consul**, Grote Markt 9, Antwerp, **T** 03-233 1608; **United States Embassy**, Regentlaan 27, Brussels, **T** 02-508 2111.

Credit card lines
If you lose your credit card, call **Card Stop**, **T** 070-344 344. For Visa in Belgium, **T** 0800-18397.

Dentists
In the Belgian Yellow Pages, www.goudengids.be, search for *tandarts* and Antwerpen/Gent. Emergencies: **T** 03-448 0220 (Antwerp); **T** 09-272 85 66 (Ghent).

Disabled
Disabled Information Advice, Holstraat 123, Ghent, **T** 09-234 0580, www.hintoostvlaanderen.be. The tourist offices in Ghent and Antwerp can also provide disabled visitors with relevant information regarding sights, restaurants and accommodation.

Doctors
Emergency, **T** 100. For the doctor on duty, **T** 03-329 5854 in Antwerp (weekends **T** 03-286 1186) or **T** 09-236 5000 in Ghent. To find the nearest doctor, visit www.havac.be.

Electricity
Belgium functions on the continental 220V mains supply.

Emergency numbers
Police **T** 101. Fire and ambulance **T** 100. European emergency number: **T** 112.

Hospitals
Antwerp: **Sint-Vincentiusziekenhuis**, Sint-Vincentiusstraat 20 (near the Stadspark), **T** 03-285 2000, www.st-vincentius.be.

Ghent: **Universitair Ziekenhuis Gent**, De Pintelaan 185, **T** 09-240 2111, www.uzgent.be.

Internet access
For details of **WiFi** hot spots in Belgium, visit www.sinfilo.com.

Antwerp: **2Zones**, Wolstraat 15, **T** 03-232 2400, www.2zones.be; **Game Mania**, Sint-Jacobsmarkt 36, **T** 03-227 3838, www.gamemania.be; **Outpost**, Beggaardenstraat 6, **T** 03-231 5456, www.outpost.be.

Ghent: **Call Center-Internet Shop**, Brabantdam 99, **T** 09-223 6802; **Coffee Lounge**, Botermarkt, **T** 09-329 3911; **City Library**, Vlaanderenplein 40, **T** 09-266 7027; **Globetrotter**, Kortrijkse-poortstraat 180, **T** 09-269 0860; **The Net**, Nederkouter 73, **T** 09-269 0053.

Language schools
Huis van het Nederlands Antwerpen, Langstraat 102, **T** 03-270 3930, recommends courses and schools. **Antwerp University Language Centre**, Universiteitsplein 1, **T** 03-820 2788. **Berlitz**, Britselei 15, **T** 03-237 1750 (Antwerp) and Kouter 177, **T** 09-233 0474 (Ghent).

Left luggage
There are facilities at Centraal and Berchem stations (Antwerp) and Sint-Pietersstation (Ghent).

Directory

Lost property

Telephone the police: **T** 0800-12312. In Ghent call police, **T** 09-266 69 14 or **Dienst Gevonden and Verloren** (lost and found), **T** 09-266 69 35.

Media

English-language **newspapers** are usually available on the day, though not always in the final edition. Cable **television** is ubiquitous, so you will generally have a choice of 30 or more channels: there is, however, no national broadcaster, with separate corporations offering programmes in Dutch (VRT) and French (RTBF), as well as several commercial channels and, handily, BBC1 and BBC2. You'll also pick up Dutch and French channels, as well as German and Italian, plus BBC World, CNN and Sky News as standard.

The free Dutch-language **weekly magazines** *Zone 03* (Antwerp) and *Zone 09* (Ghent) have features, interviews and comprehensive listings; they are prominently displayed all over the two cities. *Steps* (Antwerp) is also useful, though more advertising-led. Weekly agendas for what's on in the two cities, www.weekup.be, are available in tourist offices, hotels and some shops and restaurants. The best English-language option is *The Bulletin*, published weekly in Brussels and aimed primarily at expats in the capital: its *What's On* section offers extensive Antwerp listings.

Pharmacies

Visit www.apotheek.be for the addresses of pharmacies in Belgium. Pharmacists on duty outside office hours are displayed on pharmacy doors; for options between 2200 and 0900, **T** 0900-10500 (Antwerp) or **T** 09-236 5000 (Ghent). In Ghent, many pharmacies have condom machines outside.

Police

Antwerp: Oudaan 5, **T** 03-202 5511; **Ghent**: Belfortstraat 4, **T** 09-266 6130.

Directory

Post offices
Antwerp: Groenplaats 43, *Mon-Fri 0900-1700, Sat 0900-1200*;
Jezusstraat 26, *Mon 0900-1830, Tue-Fri 0900-1800*.
   Ghent: Stapelplein 75, *Mon-Fri 0900-1700, Sat 0900-1200*;
Lange Kruisstraat 55, *Mon-Fri 0800-1800, Sat 0900-1200*.

Public holidays
1 January, Easter and Easter Monday, 1 May, Ascension Day (6th
Thursday after Easter), Whit Sunday and Whit Monday (7th Sunday
and Monday after Easter), 21 July (National Day), 15 August
(Assumption), 1 November (All Saints Day), 11 November
(Armistice), 25 December.

Religious services
Times are posted outside churches. Belgium is a Catholic country,
but for Protestant services in Antwerp, go to **St Boniface**,
Grétrystraat 39, **T** 03-239 3339, Sunday 1030 (in English); in Ghent,
go to **Brabantdamkerk**, Sint-Kristoffelstraat 1, or the
Rabotkerk, Begijnhoflaan 31, both Sunday 1000.

Student organizations
AIESEC: Antwerp University, Prinsstraat 13, **T** 03-2204025,
www.aiesecua.be; Hoveniersberg 24, Ghent, www.aiesec.org
/belgium/gent. **Erasmus Student Network**: Antwerp University,
Prinsstraat 13, **T** 03-220 4547, www.esnantwerp.be;
Studenthouse De Brug, Sint-Pietersnieuwstraat 45, Ghent,
T 09-264 7092), www.users.pandora.be/supernick/ESN.

Taxis
See p26.

Telephone
The prefix for Belgium is +32. Dial the full area code when phoning internally, even within the city, but drop the first zero when calling from abroad. Public telephones take only calling cards, available from newsagents. For directory enquiries in English, call **T** 1407 or **T** 1404 (international). For details of prepaid mobile phone cards, visit www.base.be, www.mobistar.be or www.proximus.be.

Time
Central European Time: GMT +1 in winter, +2 in summer.

Tipping
It's customary to round up the bill and, when happy, to pay up to 15% tip. If possible, leave cash.

Toilets
Antwerp: Centraal station and Steenplein 1a (under the bridge).
Ghent: tourist office, Design Museum and Groot Vleeshuis.

Transport enquiries
Airports: Antwerp (**T** 03-285 6500, www.antwerpairport.be); Brussels National (**T** 02-753 7753, www.brusselsairport.be); Charleroi (www.charleroi-airport.com). **Eurolines coaches**: Van Stralenstraat 8, Antwerp, **T** 03-233 8662; Koningin Elisabethlaan 73, Ghent **T** 09-220 9024; www.eurolines.be.
Railway stations: for all enquiries, contact NMBS, **T** 02-528 2828, www.nmbs.be. **Marinas**: Willemdok, Godefriduskaai 99, **T** 03-231 5066, www.jachthaven-antwerpen.be; Marina Antwerpen LO, Thonetlaan 133, **T** 03-219 0895, www.jachthaven-antwerpen.be.
Trams and buses: De Lijn, **T** 070-220200 (Antwerp), **T** 09-210 9443 (Ghent), www.delijn.be.

Travel agents

Direct Line City Breaks, 12/16 Addiscombe Road, Croydon, CRO OXT, UK, **T** 0870-167 2277, www.directline-citybreaks.co.uk. Eurostar city breaks to Antwerp and Ghent. **Gold Crest Holidays**, Holiday House, Valley Drive, Ilkley, LS29 8PB, **T** 0870-700 0007, www.gold-crest.com. Ghent is included in a five-day trip to the Netherlands and Belgium. **Great Escapes**, Serenity Holidays Ltd, Cutter House, 1560 Parkway, Solent Business Park, Fareham, Hampshire, UK, PO15 7AG, **T** 0845-330 2057, www.great escapes.co.uk. Short breaks to Belgium and the Netherlands, including Antwerp and Ghent. The website lists upcoming events in these cities. **Leisure Direction**, Image House, Station Road, Totteham Hale, London N17 9LR, **T** 020-8324 4050, www.leisuredirection.co.uk. Tours to Ghent. **Martin Randall Travel**, Voysey House, Barley Mow Passage, London W4 4GF, UK, **T** 020 8742 3355, www.martinrandall.com, organizes tours to Flanders specializing in Flemish painting, with stays in Antwerp, Bruges, Brussels and Ghent. **Shortbreaks**, **T** 0870-027 6002. One of the only operators offering dedicated tours to Antwerp and Ghent, with fine hotels thrown in.

A sprint through history

4th-5th century AD	Frankish tribes make their first settlements on the River Scheldt.
7th century	Ghent develops around two abbeys, St Peter's and St Bavo's.
800	Charlemagne is crowned Holy Roman Emperor by the Pope.
843	Treaty of Verdun: Charlemagne's empire is split, with Ghent falling in French territory and the area of present-day Antwerp in German.
867	Ghent's Gravensteen castle is erected.
900	Antwerp is built on the ruins of a Viking settlement.
1008	Antwerp becomes a city.
13th century	Bruges, Ghent and Ypres thrive thanks to the cloth trade with England.
1300	Philip the Fair of France annexes Flanders.
1302	Battle of the Golden Spurs: Flemish peasants and weavers defeat French knights.
1384	Philip the Bold, Duke of Burgundy, inherits Flanders thanks to his marriage to Margaret of Maele, daughter of the last Count of Flanders. His son, Philip the Good, pursues a policy of peaceful expansion via marriage, money and machinations.
15th century	The River Zwin begins to silt up, choking Bruges's access to the sea.
1453	Philip the Good suppresses a rebellion in Ghent, forcing the city burghers to wear nooses round their necks as a punishment.

1477	Charles the Bold dies. His daughter Marie's marriage to Maximilian of Austria in 1482 sees the Low Countries pass from Burgundian to Habsburg rule.
1500	Habsburg heir Philip the Fair and his Spanish wife have a son, Charles V. Born in Ghent, he becomes ruler of Spain and its colonies, as well as the Low Countries and the Holy Roman Empire.
1505	The Fuggers of Augsburg, powerful German bankers, move their business from Bruges to Antwerp, confirming the city's status as the region's leading port and trading centre.
1540	Charles ends a revolt in Ghent by demolishing St Bavo's Abbey, replacing it with a citadel.
1550	Charles passes the Edict of Blood, condemning all heretics to death.
1555	Charles abdicates, retiring to a monastery. His possessions pass to Philip II, whose repressive anti-Protestant policies provoke iconoclastic riots.
1567	Philip sends the Duke of Alva to Flanders to suppress the Calvinists. He establishes the Council of Blood, executing 12,000, but fails to quell the revolt.
1576	Unpaid soldiers ravage Antwerp, killing thousands in the Spanish Fury. The rebel Dutch leader, William the Silent, forces Philip II to sign the Pacification of Ghent, guaranteeing freedom of belief.
1581	The northern territories, led by William, reject Philip II and sign the Union of Utrecht, which incorporates Antwerp.
1585	Antwerp falls to the Spanish after a brutal siege.

1599	Archduke Albert and his wife, Philip II's daughter Isabel, assume power in the Spanish Netherlands.
17th century	The so-called Golden Age, era of Rubens and the Counter-Reformation. In reality, the Flemish cities fall into decline as Protestant cloth workers and merchants flee to England and Holland.
1648	The Treaty of Münster ends a century of religious conflict and recognizes the Netherlands. However, the Scheldt is blocked by the Dutch, forcing Antwerp into two centuries of decline.
1701-13	The War of the Spanish Succession results in the Southern Netherlands passing to the Austrian Habsburgs. They do little to better the fortunes of Antwerp or Ghent.
1780	Joseph II of Austria's reforms prove unpopular, leading to revolts against his rule in 1789. A short-lived constitution of the United Belgian States is drawn up before the Austrians regain control.
1795	Belgium is annexed by France, French becomes the official language and the division between the French-speaking elite and the poorer Dutch-speakers grows. Napoleon develops Antwerp's docks for military ends.
1800	Lieven Bauwens smuggles a spinning jenny from England to Ghent, kick-starting the city's economy.
1815	After Waterloo, the Congress of Vienna creates a united realm of the northern and southern Low Countries under Dutch Protestant rule.
1830	The Belgian revolution begins in Brussels on 25 August; independence is declared on 4 October.

1831	Belgium invites Leopold of Saxe-Coburg, a German relation of the British royal family, to become King of the Belgians. Antwerp undergoes a building boom.
1863	Antwerp regains free use of the Scheldt, resulting in rapid economic growth.
1865	Leopold's ruthlessly ambitious son, Leopold II, takes control. The Flemish movement gathers pace, Dutch becoming an official language alongside French.
1885	Leopold II establishes a private kingdom in the Congo, exploiting its natural resources mercilessly. Following international outcry, he is forced to hand over control of the territory to the state in 1908.
1909	Leopold dies; his nephew, Albert, takes the throne.
1913	Ghent hosts the World Fair. Many medieval buildings are restored and neo-Gothic buildings erected.
1914	Despite Belgium's neutral status in the First World War, the Kaiser's army invades and occupies most of the country. King Albert I holds a stretch of land by the coast throughout the war, during which many Flemish towns are razed to the ground. The term 'Flanders Fields' comes to encapsulate the scale and pointlessness of the slaughter.
1920	Antwerp hosts the seventh Olympic Games.
1934	Albert dies and his son, Leopold III, succeeds him.
1940	Germany invades Belgium on 10 May. Leopold III swiftly capitulates, provoking fury among his compatriots and leading to the evacuation of British forces at Dunkirk. During the occupation, 25,000 Jews are sent from Belgium to the concentration camps; just 1200 survive.

Background

1944	Antwerp is liberated on 3 September, Ghent on 5 September. Antwerp's port becomes crucial as a supply line for the Allied advance; the battle to secure access to the Scheldt rages until 8 November. More than 1000 V-2 rockets hit Antwerp.
1945	Germany surrenders on 8 May. After the war, 87,000 Belgians are prosecuted for treason, war crimes or collaboration, some members of the Flemish and Walloon SS brigades. About 4000 receive death sentences, 241 of which are carried out.
1946	Leopold III is exonerated from treason. However, he has lost the trust of his people.
1948	Belgian women get the right to vote.
16 Jul 1951	Leopold abdicates, and is succeeded by his son, Baudouin.
25 Mar 1957	Belgium becomes one of six members of the EEC, the forerunner to the European Union.
1960	The Congo becomes an independent state.
1970-94	Constitutional reforms introduce and refine the administrative regions of Flanders, Wallonia and Brussels, as well as the French-speaking and Flemish communities. Each of these administrations has a degree of autonomy.
1993	Antwerp is European Cultural Capital.
31 Jul 1993	Baudouin dies, sparking an outcry of national mourning; his brother, Albert II, becomes king.
1 Jan 1999	Belgium joins the Euro.
1999	General election: the far-right Vlaams Blok wins 30% of the vote in Antwerp and Mechelen.

Sinjoors

They say Antwerpenaars are always complaining, yet they have long had a knack for making the best of things. In the 16th century, the Spanish occupiers took to calling them 'Señors'. This was almost certainly sarcastic – "Well, señor, who the hell do you think you are?" – but the locals soon began to call themselves 'Sinjoors', as if it were the biggest mark of respect in the world.

The term has even come to define whether you can call yourself a real Antwerpenaar. This is perhaps the only city in the world where you can only be a true local if you and both your parents were born there: sorry, Rubens, but you don't make the grade. Those unlucky souls from beyond Antwerp are called *pagader*, or 'little children', a reference to the Spanish soldiers who were not big and fit enough to fight, and were given the job of collecting taxes in the city.

Some say such terms illustrate the city's fabled chauvinism, a tendency that the Dutch-speaking Belgian author Eric de Kuyper touches on in his autobiographical novel *Hotel Solitude*: "I must admit that I've tried to love the town and I thought I hadn't succeeded. Recently, I suddenly realised that I had loved the town a lot after all. In particular, I realised how I was waiting as a lover does for a glimpse of reciprocal love, no matter how brief. In vain. Recognition failed to come. The town continued to revel in its fierce xenophobia. I was and remained the stranger, the one who cannot, does not want to and even is not allowed to speak its language. The town made it clear that I was a whore-hopper, an outsider."

It's a sentiment recognized by Ronnie Dusoir of the Plantin-Moretus Museum, a thoroughbred Sinjoor. "Antwerpenaars," he says, "consider everyone who doesn't master their unique dialect – which they call 'language' – to be peasants. All other 'provincials' would say they are pretentious, swollen-headed and pompous… To which Antwerpenaars habitually reply, 'We can't help it. Antwerp is the greatest city in the world'."

In fact, it is often the outsiders, the love-struck *pagaders*, who make the wildest claims for it. In the 16th century, a Dutch linguist, Johannes Goropius Becanus, announced that the Antwerp tongue was the oldest language on earth, that the names Adam and Eve derived from Aardman and Eeuwvat, and that the Garden of Eden was located in the Antwerp area.

According to the writer and former city poet Tom Lanoye, the best way to understand 'Sinjoordom' is to go back to the 16th century, when Antwerp was a dynamic, bustling centre, full of aspiration and reaching out to the world. The fall of Antwerp to Spanish troops in 1585 triggered a drastic brain drain, with more than half of the city's inhabitants fleeing to the northern Lowlands, taking their skills and knowledge with them. (Some citizens shake their heads sadly when this topic comes up, as if the city were still feeling the effects today.)

Centuries on, says Lanoye, Antwerpenaars cannot stop feeling important: "But they are also mortified and bitter, just like some British people feel sour about the loss of empire. At the same time, they do have a lot to be proud of." The commercial, cultural and political centre of Flanders, Antwerp is a wannabe capital – but, of course, Brussels is the political capital, and that hurts. "There's a feeling of being overlooked," Lanoye concludes.

It hurts, too, that so many of the city's high achievers are not Sinjoors. Lanoye is from Sint-Niklaas; the current city poet was born in Rotterdam; even Rubens, the city's most famous citizen, was born in Germany. "Antwerp", says the author Anne Provoost (born in tiny Poperinge, in case you were wondering), "has always been a city of newcomers. Sometimes I worry that Antwerpenaars forget that. We are all 'immigrants' in this city. We were welcomed here, or our parents or grandparents were. Hospitality is what made them stay."

Patrick Janssens, the city's dynamic socialist mayor – at least until the elections in October 2006 – prefers to dwell on the positive side of Sinjoordom. "A Sinjoor," he says, "is someone who enjoys life in every detail, which means he is sometimes distracted and lacking in ambition. But Sinjoors have true character, and this is what others envy."

While Antwerpenaars embrace new trends, Gentenaars are seen as rather more modest and, perhaps, more content, if not complacent at times. However, Ghent's rebellious streak has made it a hotbed of progressive and socialist politics, something Antwerp's liberals must be deeply envious of right now. Antwerp, with its restless appetite for flamboyance, is famous for theatre; inward-looking Ghent, for music. Antwerp is commercial, Ghent more poetic, more quietly artistic.

If you strike up a conversation with an Antwerpenaar, wherever they are from, you will probably be struck by their lack of pretension, despite all their claims to grandeur. For a city of fashion and design, Antwerp is remarkably down-to-earth; and, for all their swaggering, Sinjoors don't take themselves too seriously. As one (envious?) visitor from the Netherlands observed: "They still know how to linger over a beer; they know how to have fun …"

Malcontent? Sometimes. Complex? Yes. Vain? Certainly. Overambitious? Well, look at Cogels-Osylei, the ultimate in delusions of grandeur. The result, however, is architectural splendour that everyone can enjoy. After all, a spot of vanity never ruined a city…

Books

Contemporary fiction in translation

Claus, H, (tr Pomerans, J), *The Sorrow of Belgium* (2003), Overlook Press. One of Belgium's greatest novels, a complex but faithful portrayal of West Flanders during and after the Second World War.
Mortier, E, *Marcel* (2003), Vintage. Compassionate, elegantly written exploration of the bitter history of Flemish collaboration during the Nazi occupation, through the eyes of an observant boy.

Mortier, E, *My Fellow Skin* (2003), Harvill. A boyhood awakening to homosexuality, set against Flanders' drizzle-coated landscape.
Provoost, A, *Falling* (1997), Ark Fiction. Disturbing story of a teenage boy's descent into racism.
Provoost, A, *In the Shadow of the Ark* (2005), Simon and Schuster. A vivid retelling of the Biblical account of the Flood, which asks why a merciful God should choose only some people to survive.
Verhulst, D, *Problemski Hotel* (2005), Marion Boyars. Searing depiction of western attitudes to refugees, inspired by the author's stay in an asylum-seekers' centre.

Fiction by anglophone authors

Hollinghurst, A, *The Folding Star* (1994), Vintage. The Booker-winning author set this tale of a middle-aged academic's obsession with a 17-year-old student in Flanders.
Magdaelen, I I, Emma H (2003), The Toby Press. Crime story about a beautiful Flemish girl shot as a collaborator after the war.
Royle, N, *Antwerp* (2004), Serpent's Tail. Thriller involving prostitution, cult Belgian cinema and the painter Paul Delvaux, exploiting the city's sleazier side.
Sarton, M, *The Bridge of Years* (1997), The Women's Press. Finely written novel about a Belgian family in the interwar period.

Classic Flemish literature

Boon, P L, *Chapel Road* (1972), Dalkey Archive. Via the life of 'heroine' Ondine in a Flemish town, this irreverent, structurally complex modernist novel explores the birth and development of socialism.
Conscience, H, *The Lion of Flanders* (1881), Burns & Oates. Patriotic novel about the Flemish defeat of the French at the Battle of the Golden Spurs in 1302.

De Coster, C, *The Legend of the Glorious Adventures of Tyl Ulenspiegel in the Land of Flanders and Elsewhere* (1978), Journeyman Press. A wise fool and prankster wanders through 16th-century Flanders.

Elsschot, W, *Cheese* (2002), Granta. Hilarious Antwerp satire about a shipping clerk who suddenly finds himself the Luxembourg importer of Edam, but fails to shift a single ball.

Elsschot, W, *Villa des Roses* (2003), Granta. A tale of a life in a Parisian boarding house, it exposes human weaknesses in deceptively savage fashion.

Maeterlinck, M, *Hothouses: Poems, 1889* (2003), Princeton University Press. Belgium's only Nobel Price winner for literature.

Rodenbach, G, *Bruges-la-Morte* (2005), Dedalus. Poetic, gloomy Symbolist novel (1892) about a bereaved widower who chooses Bruges as an appropriate place for his grief.

Non-fiction

Blyth, D, *Flemish Cities Explored* (1998), Pallas Athene. Beautifully written peregrinations in six Flemish cities including Antwerp and Ghent.

Crane, N, *Mercator* (2003), Phoenix. Lively biography of the Flemish cartographer, the father of modern map-making.

Geyl, P, *History of the Dutch-Speaking Peoples 1555-1648* (2001), Phoenix Press. Classic, crisply written account of a century of religious ferment in the Low Countries.

Haex, P, and **Heirman**, F, *Antwerp F-A-Q* (2004), De Geus. In-depth, alternative guide in Dutch.

Naegels, T, *Wandelgids Antwerpen Boekenstad* (2004), Lannoo. Excellent series of walks through literary Antwerp (in Dutch).

Roels, H, and **Vermeir**, S, *Zurenborg Belle Epoque* (1996), Pandora. Cogels-Osylei gets the coffee-table treatment.

Language

To talk about 'Flemish' is to wade into a sea of mud. Some say there is no such thing as Flemish, only Dutch; others protest that there definitely is, given the long tradition of written works in Flemish dialect. Technically speaking, 'Flemish' refers to the Dutch dialects spoken in Belgium, sometimes known as 'southern Dutch'. In general, these dialects favour older words than 'Dutch' Dutch, and the pronunciation is less guttural, softer and, well, sexier. And think twice before dusting off your schoolboy French: some Antwerpenaars delight in snubbing visitors from the Hexagon ("Parlez-vous francais?", enquired an earnest group of Routard-wielding backpackers in one central restaurant. "Non," came the reply). That said, the Antwerp dialect contains Gallicisms such as *soigné* (to be well looked after, a term you hear to describe service in a restaurant) and you may hear people saying "*merci*." In Ghent, there are even more Gallicisms, notably "*salut*" – although here, it means goodbye...

Pronunciation
One distinctive quality of the hard, nasal Antwerp dialect is the long flat 'aaa' vowel sound. It takes a lot of effort to pronounce it, which is why the locals are often described as having big mouths. East Flemish is spoken in Ghent, a place with its own linguistic peculiarity: that of mainly older Gentenaars pronouncing dialect words with a 'posh' French accent, which can be truly disorientating. To find out more, visit www.lowlands-l.net or www.vereniging.leuven.be/SBD.

Basic words and phrases

thank you	*dank u*
thank you very much	*dank u wel*
hello	*hallo*
good morning	*goedemorgen*

good evening	*goedenavond*
goodbye	*dag*
yes	*ja*
no	*nee*
please	*alstublieft*
Excuse me!	*Pardon!*
Do you speak English?	*Spreekt U Engels?*
I don't know	*Ik weet het niet*
Where is….?	*Waar is…..?*
Can you help me?	*Kunt U mij helpen?*
How much does….cost?	*Hoeveel kost het?*
When does…open/close?	*Wanneer gaat … open/dicht?*
I would like	*Ik wil graag*
One ticket, please	*Een kaartje, alstublieft*
Two tickets, please	*Twee kaartes, alstublieft*

Emergencies

Help!	*Help!*
Where is the police station?	*Waar is het politiebureau?*
I'm unwell	*Ik ben onwel*
I need a doctor	*Ik heb een arts nodig*

Getting around/recognizing signs

exit	*uitruit* [when driving]
way out	*uitgang*
street	*straat*
square	*plein*
boulevard	*leie*
quay	*kaai*

Days of the week

Monday	*maandag*
Tuesday	*dinsdag*
Wednesday	*woensdag*

Background

Thursday	*donderdag*
Friday	*vrijdag*
Saturday	*zaterdag*
Sunday	*zondag*

Numbers

one	*één*
two	*twee*
three	*drie*
four	*vier*
five	*vijf*
six	*zes*
seven	*zeven*
eight	*acht*
nine	*negen*
ten	*tien*

Food and drink glossary

Food

aardappelkroketten	potato croquettes
appelmoes	apple sauce
balletjes	little meatballs
boterhammen	sandwiches
botersausje	butter sauce
brood	bread
champignons	mushrooms
chocoladesaus	chocolate sauce
dagschotel	dish of the day (ie, a lunchtime spccial)
dagsoep	soup of the day
eend	duck
filet américaine	prepared raw mince (not steak!)

frieten	chips
garnalen	grey North Sea shrimps
garnalkroketten	prawn croquettes
gebakken	baked
gefrituurde	fried
gegrilde	grilled
gemarineerde	marinated
gestoomde	steamed
groenten	vegetables
hesp	ham
hoofdgerechten	main courses
huisgemaakt	home-made
kaas	cheese
kaaskroketten	cheese croquettes
kabeljauw	cod
kip	chicken
knoflook	garlic
lamsvlees	lamb
lookboter	garlic butter
meloen	melon
nagerechten	desserts
notensla	rocket salad
oesters	oysters
pannekoeken met ijs	pancakes with ice cream
ribbekes	ribs
rundvlees	beef
spek	bacon
spinazie	spinach
sla	salad
slagroom	cream
tomaat	tomato
tonijn	tuna
tuinkruiden	garden herbs
vanillesaus	vanilla sauce
varkensvlees	pork

vegetarische gerechten	vegetarian dishes
vis	fish
vlees	meat
voor de kleintjes	for children
voorgerechten	starters
wafel met suiker/slagroom	waffle with sugar/whipped cream
wijnsaus	wine sauce
witloof	chicory
zalm	salmon
zeetong	sole

Drinks

alcoholvrije bier	alcohol-free beer
aperitieven	aperitifs
appel/appelsap	apple/apple juice
borrelhapjes	savoury snacks
bruisend/plat	sparkling/flat water
cafeinevrij	caffeine-free
cecemel	cold chocolate milk
frisdranken	cold drinks
kappertjes	capers
lait russe	milky coffee
oranje/sinaasappel	orange/orange juice
pompelmoes	grapefruit
portie bitterballen	little meat croquettes
portie zwarte/groene olijven	portion of black/green olives
sterke dranken	spirits
vers sinaasappelsap	fresh orange juice
warme dranken	hot drinks
wijn/rood/rose/wit/huis	wine/red/rose/white/house
wijnen	wine

Index

Credits

Footprint credits

Text editor: Sarah Thorowgood
Editorial: Sophie Blacksell, Felicity Laughton, Angus Dawson, Lorna Broomfield
Map editor: Sarah Sorensen
Picture editor: Robert Lunn
Publisher: Patrick Dawson
In-house cartography: Kevin Feeney
Proof-reading: Sarah Sorensen
Design: Mytton Williams
Maps: Footprint Handbooks Ltd

Photography credits

Front cover: Marc Romanelli/Alamy (Silvius Brabo statue). Black and white images: visitflanders.co.uk (p1 De Koninck and *genever*, p5 Lange Wapper, p31 Rubens statue, p99 gabled house) Generic images: John Matchett. Back cover: visitflanders.co.uk (Graslei, Ghent)

Print

Manufactured in India by Nutech Photolithographers, Delhi. Pulp from sustainable forests.

If you want to let us know about your experiences – good, bad or ugly – then, go to www.footprintbooks.com and send in your comments.

Publishing information

Footprint Antwerp & Ghent
1st edition
Text and maps © Footprint Handbooks Ltd October 2006

ISBN 1 904777 75 9
CIP DATA: a catalogue record for this book is available from the British Library

Published by Footprint Handbooks
6 Riverside Court
Lower Bristol Road
Bath, BA2 3DZ, UK
T +44 (0)1225 469141
F +44 (0)1225 469461
discover@footprintbooks.com
www.footprintbooks.com

Distributed in the USA by Publishers Group West

® Footprint Handbooks and the Footprint mark are a registered trademark of Footprint Handbooks Ltd

Every effort has been made to ensure that the facts contained in this pocket guide are accurate. However the author and publishers cannot accept responsibility for any loss, injury or inconvenience sustained as a result of information or advice contained in this guide.

Hotel and restaurant codes should only be taken as a guide to the prices and facilities offered by the establishment. It is at the discretion of the owners to vary them from time to time.

Complete title list

Latin America & Caribbean

Antigua & Leeward
  Islands (P)
Argentina
Barbados (P)
Bolivia
Brazil
Caribbean Islands
Chile
Costa Rica
Cuba
Cuzco & the Inca Heartland
Discover Belize,
  Guatemala & Southern
  Mexico
Discover Patagonia
Discover Peru, Bolivia
  & Ecuador
Dominican Republic (P)
Ecuador & Galápagos
Mexico & Central America
Nicaragua
Peru
Rio de Janeiro (P)
South American Handbook
Venezuela

North America

New York (P)
Vancouver (P)
Discover Western Canada

Africa & the Middle East

Cape Town (P)
Dubai (P)
Egypt
Kenya
Marrakech (P)
Morocco
Namibia
South Africa
Tanzania
Tunisia

Asia

Bhutan
Borneo
Cambodia
Discover Vietnam,
  Cambodia & Laos
Goa
Hong Kong (P)
India
Indonesia
Laos
Malaysia & Singapore
Nepal
Northern Pakistan
Rajasthan
South India
Sri Lanka
Thailand
Tibet
Vietnam

Australasia

Australia
Discover East Coast Australia
New Zealand
Sydney (P)
West Coast Australia

Europe

Andalucía
Antwerp & Ghent (P)
Barcelona (P)
Belfast (P)
Berlin (P)
Bilbao (P)
Bologna (P)
Cardiff & South Wales (P)
Copenhagen (P)
Costa de la Luz (P)
Croatia
Dublin (P)
Edinburgh (P)
Glasgow (P)
England
Ireland

Lisbon (P)
London
London (P)
Madrid (P)
Naples (P)
Northern Spain
Paris (P)
Reykjavik (P)
Scotland
Scotland Highlands
  & Islands
Seville (P)
Siena & the heart
  of Tuscany (P)
Spain
Tallinn (P)
Turin (P)
Valencia (P)
Turkey
Valencia (P)
Verona (P)

Lifestyle guides

Diving the World
European City Breaks
Snowboarding the World
Surfing Britain
Surfing Europe
Surfing the World

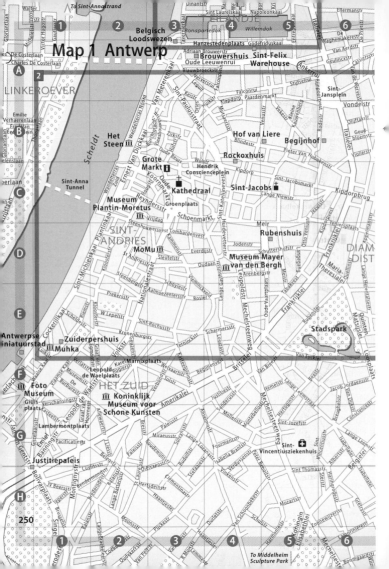

Map 1 Antwerp

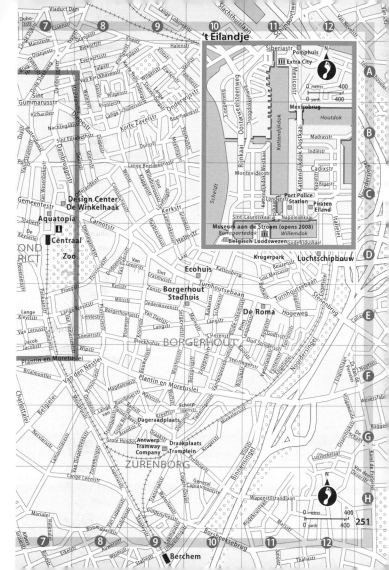

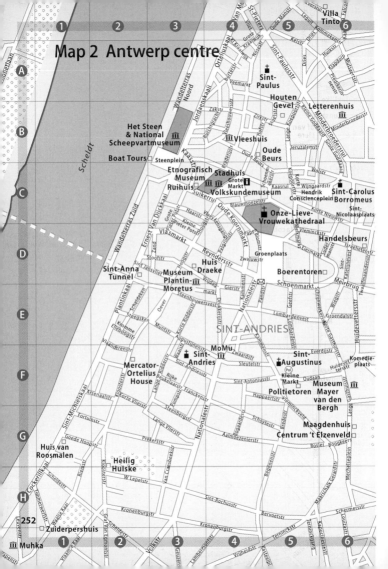

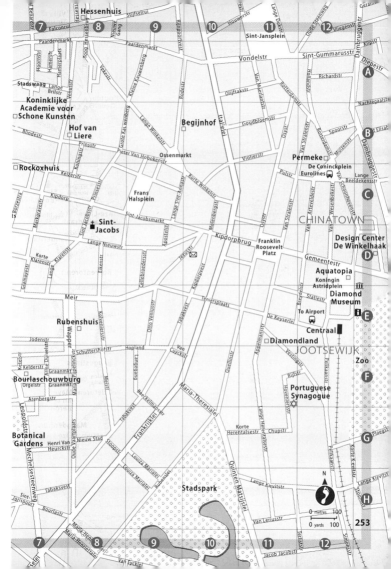

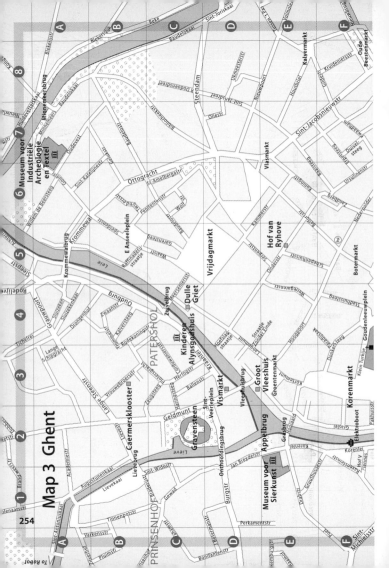

Map 3 Ghent

254

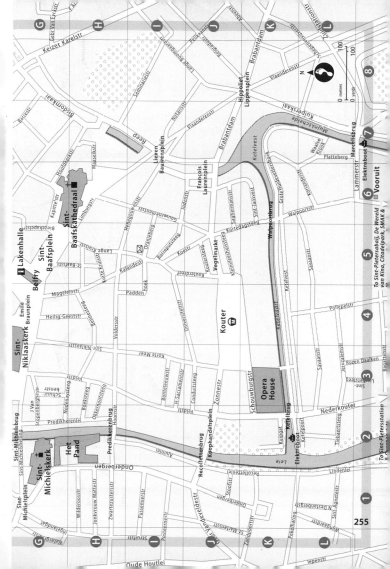

255